D1472588

This special edition of the Food Editors' Favorites: Desserts was made to benefit MADD and increase your awareness of our work.

Before enjoying the many recipes that follow, please take a few minutes to read over the material. It explains MADD's history and the services MADD performs. After reading these few pages, you will understand better why MADD is necessary and how you can support this bold cause.

It is estimated that two out of every five Americans will be involved in an alcohol-related crash in their lifetime. On average, 65 people die and 1,534 are injured each and every day as a result of alcohol and other drug-related driving crashes. Hopefully, through your support and involvement in the efforts of MADD, we can create a future that is less violent for us all.

Mothers Against Drunk Driving ™

"Mothers Against Drunk Driving mobilizes victims and their allies to establish the public conviction that drunk driving is unacceptable and criminal, in order to promote corresponding public policies, programs and personal accountability."

MADD was founded in Fair Oaks, California in 1980. An aggressive campaign resulted in California passing the toughest drunk driving laws in the country at that time.

This astounding success on the West Coast was only the beginning. Shortly thereafter, MADD erupted from a one-woman organization to a nationwide, non-profit corporation with more than a million supporters and members. Thousands of women and men are active volunteers in over 385 chapters in 48 states. Affiliates are active in Canada, Sweden, Ireland, Australia, New Zealand and Great Britain.

Numerous successes fuel the MADD operation, both at the National Office in Texas and in communities scattered throughout America. Since 1981, over 950 drunk driving laws have been enacted nationwide. The rights of victims and survivors of alcohol-related crashes are now being viewed more equitably in a criminal justice system which, only a few years ago, made the rights of the intoxicated driver a priority. Youth programs affiliated with MADD have sprung up in almost every state, providing teenagers with a sound background in alcohol awareness and education.

MADD's Community Programs

MADD develops new ideas and programs to increase the unacceptability of drunk driving, and attempts to involve all Americans — especially our youth — in solving the problem. Some of our ongoing programs include:

Public Awareness Campaigns

Throughout the year, MADD promotes public awareness to raise the nation's consciousness of alcohol and other drug-impaired driving. MADD has direct contact with major print and broadcast media, and in local communities. Special public awareness campaigns are conducted throughout the year. These and other initiatives are MADD's most important tools for prompting people to be responsible in their actions.

_K.I.S.S._ MADD introduced "Keep It a Safe Summer" (K.I.S.S.) in an effort to make Americans more aware of the dangers of drinking and driving—on the road or on the water. This three-month summer safety program, which begins on Memorial Day and concludes on Labor Day, promotes personal responsibility through a far-reaching public awareness effort. The primary vehicle of K.I.S.S. is a "Family Vacation Pack" that condenses all the program material into a handy reference package for those who need it most: summer travelers.

Drive For Life: A month-long campaign focuses attention and educates Americans about the tragedy of alcohol and other drug-related driving. Drive For Life culminates the Saturday before Labor Day. Americans are asked to drive with the headlights turned on during Drive for Life Day.

Designated Driver: MADD promotes designated driver programs. Having a designated driver in a group means having a sober driver available to get everyone home safely. safely.

PROJECT RED RIBBON: An extensive public awareness campaign developed by MADD to urge Americans not to drink and drive through the holiday season. PROJECT RED RIBBON intends to change the meaning of "tie one on" by asking citizens across the country to tie a red ribbon to their vehicles as a symbol of their commitment not to drink and drive. The red ribbon also symbolizes hope for a safe holiday season.

Candlelight Vigils: Each year MADD conducts Candlelight Vigils of Remembrance and Hope—remembrance of loved ones killed or injured in drunk driving crashes, and hope for a less violent future for us all.

Youth Education Programs

MADD has developed specific programs to reduce the prevalence of drinking and the incidence of drunk driving among America's youth. Components are being designed to enhance student-parent dialogue, and to provide skills training to show young people how to avoid dangerous situations involving alcohol and drug use.

Operation Prom/Graduation: This is a major community awareness program to ensure that prom and graduation nights are memorable occasions, and not memorial ones. Operation Prom/Graduation includes widespread media, contests, and visual reminders for students about the dangers of drinking and driving.

Nationwide Poster/Essay Contest: This national competition offers students in grades 1-12 the opportunity to exercise their creative writing and artistic skills to deliver a strong message about the problems of combining alcohol and drugs with driving. Local student winners compete at the national level for awards and public recognition.

MADD *Student Library:* To meet the needs of countless students who request information about teenage drunk driving, MADD publishes the *Student Library.*

Student Organizations: MADD offers guidance and detailed advice to high school students who are interested in organizing student groups to combat teenage impaired driving. Student leaders receive ideas for ongoing projects and programs to educate their peers and elevate their awareness about the disproportionate number of alcohol-related crashes caused by teenagers driving under the influence of alcohol and other drugs.

"Be Smart! Don't Start!": MADD is a national sponsor and participant in this nationwide campaign aimed at preventing the use of alcohol by youth *before* they face increased peer and societal pressure to drink. There are two target audiences: 1) preteens, ages 8-12 years old; and 2) adults who influence attitudes and behaviors of children—especially parents, teachers and physicians.

FREE FOR LIFE: A refusal skills development program which teaches junior high school youth how to resist peer pressure to use alcohol and other drugs. The program relies on "peer education" techniques, having the students themselves plan and lead class discussions.

Speakers Bureaus

MADD chapters across America offer trained speakers to address civic and professional organizations, community groups, legislatures, public and private industries, schools and other concerned citizens. These knowledgeable leaders provide innovative lectures and educational information, concerning critical traffic safety issues such as legislation, victims rights, community actions programs; and prevention techniques to remove intoxicated drivers from our highways.

Case/Court Monitoring

MADD's ongoing case/court monitoring program monitors the enforcement and legal process for DWI's in communities across America. Specifically, MADD volunteers monitor DWI arrests and cases being adjudicated in order to advise the public whether DWI laws, as well as enforcement, prosecution and defense are adequate.

MADD's
Legislative Goals

Since 1981, tremendous progress has been made at both the state and federal level in passing tougher anti-drunk driving legislation. However, there is still so much to do. This year, our legislative efforts will focus primarily on the following issues:

Victim Compensation. In keeping with the MADD objective of aiding victims of drunk driving crashes, MADD advocates that state governments provide a source of compensation funds for the financial losses and expenses of injured DWI victims and their families. At present, 45 states have established such programs, which provide crucial assistance for the victims who make application for funds.

Victim Bill of Rights. A Victim Bill of Rights provides a legislative means to ensure that victims of alcohol-related crashes have guaranteed rights within the criminal justice system. For many years such rights were disregarded in the effort to insure the rights of the accused, but it is increasingly recognized that the victim must also be accorded such protections as the right to describe the impact of the crime on his or her life and to be informed of developments in the adjudication process. In some states, a Bill of Rights has been established in comprehensive form, while in others, victim rights have been passed in individual laws. To date, 44 states have passed some version of a Victim Bill of Rights.

Administrative Revocation. Administrative license revocation is a procedure to suspend, at the time of arrest, the driving privileges of persons caught driving with an illegal concentration of alcohol in their bodies. Studies have shown that license suspension or revocation is one of the most effective sanctions in reducing subsequent crashes, and administrative revocation proves even more effective. By suspending the license at the time of the offense several objectives are accomplished: the impaired driver is subjected to the consequences of his/her actions immediately instead of six months or more later; the risk of repeat offenses and crashes is reduced; man hours are saved for both enforcement and adjudicative systems; and law enforcement morale often rises as efforts achieve more certain results. Currently 23 states have administrative revocation provisions.

License Plate Confiscation for Habitual Offenders. Removing license plates from habitual drunk drivers or those who drive on suspended licenses serves to prevent them from repeating their offenses. While license revocation does not provide a visible indicator of the offense, removal of license plates from vehicles makes a repeat offense apparent to law enforcement. Currently, six states have statutes providing for license plate impoundment, while others have considered or tried such procedures.

Mandatory Incarceration for Repeat Offenders. MADD favors confinement which cannot be suspended or probated for those convicted more than once of driving while under the influence. Drunk driving is a crime, and continued incidence of such offenses warrants the punitive effect of a certain jail sentence. Making the sentence mandatory removes the uncertainty and increases deterrent value of the sanction.

Open Container. MADD supports laws which prohibit any occupant of a motor vehicle from possessing an open container of alcoholic beverage. Such a statute goes beyond the effect of "don't drink and drive" ordinances, under which an officer must actually observe the offense before an arrest may be made; such statutes make it easy for a driver to hand off his or her container to a passenger.

Plastic Embossed Color-Coded Drivers' Licenses. The use of unalterable drivers' licenses which clearly indicate whether the driver is of drinking age is very important in enforcing the "21" drinking age law. Using a color code for under-drinking-age drivers facilitates identification, and utilizing a plastic-embossed license helps to forestall alteration of licenses.

Dram Shop. Dram Shop laws provide for lawsuits by alcohol-related crash victims against drinking establishments and individuals which serve alcoholic beverages to an intoxicated driver. At least 41 states have either case law or statutes concerning dram shop liability, although some of these provide specific limitations on the extent of liability.

.08 Per Se/.05 Presumptive. In 41 states, a BAC level of .10 percent is considered "per se" evidence of intoxication; in many states a set level, usually .10 percent, is also considered to be "presumptive" evidence of intoxication. Research evidence shows that people are actually impaired at lower levels, and the American Medical Association has even called for a per se level of .05 percent. MADD supports making .08 percent per se evidence of intoxication, with a presumptive level of .05 percent.

Alcohol Warning Labels. MADD has endorsed the concept of requiring warning labels on alcoholic beverages. Such warnings should state that alcohol will impair skills necessary for operation of motor vehicles or heavy machinery. The use of such warnings is consistent with similar warnings on other hazardous substances and will provide a direct opportunity to educate the public concerning the risks involved in alcohol consumption.

Self-Sufficient Drunk Driving Programs Funded by Offenders. MADD supports efforts to provide funds for drunk driving programs through fees, fines and other assessments, both to ensure a reliable source of continuing funding for effective programs and to place the burden of these programs where it belongs: on the drunken driver.

Mandatory Alcohol/Drug Testing of all Drivers in Crashes Resulting in Fatalities/Serious Injury. MADD advocates the requirement of alcohol/drug testing of all drivers in all traffic crashes resulting in fatalities or serious bodily injury.

Legislation Providing For Preliminary Breath Tests. MADD supports providing the most modern technology (Preliminary Breath Testers - PBTs) to police officers investigating drunken drivers, both to increase the efficiency of the arrest process and to protect the innocent.

MADD's
Victim Services

Each of the more than 23,900 fatalities and half a million serious injuries incurred yearly is a unique and irreplaceable individual with a name, a family, and dreams which must now go unfulfilled. Each represents far more than a faceless number to his or her family and friends, who are now caught in the tragic ripple effect set off by each crash.

For drunk driving victims — both injured persons and survivors of fatalities — MADD offers the following special services:

Crisis Intervention

Alcohol and other drug-related crashes create a critical period in the lives of victims. MADD provides emotional support to help victims cope with their grief and anger. In addition, victims receive practical information to help them understand the grieving process and their pending court cases.

Victim Support

MADD provides numerous reading materials to help victims understand their unique grieving symptoms. It also brings victims together in victims support groups to discuss their feelings and futures. Victims can offer each other a unique understanding and provide emotional support and reassurance to those who share the loss or serious injury of a loved one.

Victim Advocacy

Victims are offered a thorough explanation of the judicial process. MADD advocates clarify the victims' rights, accompany them to court when necessary and follow-up on the sentencing of the offender. MADD offers the *Victim Information Pamphlet* and *Victims' Rights in Alcohol Impaired Crashes* to inform victims about their rights in court proceedings. A new publication, the *MADDVOCATE*, provides up-to-date information for victim advocates.

Information and Referral

MADD chapters refer victims to state and local agencies which offer financial and legal information, as well as emotional assistance. Chapter members are always available to counsel and guide victims throughout the grieving process.

MADD
and You

Grassroots activism is the force of MADD. Your unyielding determination, commitment, energy, courage and creativity, along with thousands of others, is needed to reduce the number of deaths and injuries from alcohol & other drug-related driving.

You and what you do can create a future that is less violent for everyone. We invite you to be actively involved in the work to end alcohol & other drug-impaired drunk driving. Together we *can* make a difference — even create a *demand* to end drunk driving.

There are various ways to participate actively in this bold cause:

• Be responsible for your own thinking and actions about drunk driving — *don't drink and drive.*

• Support your family and friends in being responsible for their thinking and actions about drunk driving — *friends don't let friends drive drunk.*

• Be informed about the issues of drunk driving. Make yourself knowledgeable so that you can create conversations with others that raise their consciousness and support them in being responsible. MADD provides numerous written materials to educate you, we are just a telephone call away.

• Be actively involved at whatever level you can give. If your community has a MADD chapter, make your talent and time available to help. Explore the possibility of organizing a chapter in your community, if one is not established. If you prefer, work with other resources in your community to fight alcohol & other drug-related driving, or create resources that are missing.

Congratulations. Through your financial contribution, you have expressed a commitment to end alcohol & other drug-related driving. Now, take the next step — *BE ACTIVELY INVOLVED.* Contact MADD in your local community or the National Office.

MADD National Office
669 Airport Freeway, Suite 310
Hurst, Texas 76053
817/268-6233

Mothers Against Drunk Driving ™

7

FOOD EDITORS' FAVORITES

Desserts

Edited by
**Barbara Gibbs
Ostmann**
and
Jane Baker

For
The Newspaper Food
Editors and Writers
Association, Inc.

Dial Publishing Production Staff

Production Manager	Sue Sensenich
Art Director	Leigh Marovich
Proofreader	Cornelia Wells
Manuscript Preparation	Tonya Nardi

Copyright © 1988 by Dial Publishing Company

All rights reserved. No part of the book may be reproduced or utilized in any form or by any means, electronic or mechanical, including photocopying, recording, or by any information retrieval system, without permission in writing from Dial Publishing Company. Printed in the United States of America.

Contents

Contributing Food Editors

Wanda A. Adams, *Seattle Post-Intelligencer* / Seattle, Wash.
Harriet Aldridge, *Arkansas Gazette* / Little Rock, Ark.
Julian Armstrong, *The Gazette* / Montreal, Quebec, Canada
Bernie Arnold, *Nashville Banner* / Nashville, Tenn.
Lee Aschoff, *Milwaukee Sentinel* / Milwaukee, Wis.
Helen Austin, *Arkansas Democrat* / Little Rock, Ark.
Jane Baker, *The Phoenix Gazette* / Phoenix, Ariz.
Pat Baldridge, *Morning Advocate/State Times* / Baton Rouge, La.
Claire Barriger, *The Leader-Post* / Regina, Saskatchewan, Canada
Bev Bennett, *Chicago Sun-Times* / Chicago, Ill.
Marcia Bennett, *Pittsburgh Post-Gazette* / Pittsburgh, Pa.
Marie Bianco, *Newsday* / Long Island, N.Y.
Rosemary Black, *The Record* / Hackensack, N.J.
Anne Byrn, *Atlanta Journal-Constitution* / Atlanta, Ga.
Marian Burros, *The New York Times* / New York City, N.Y.
Evelyn Cairns, *News-Herald Newspapers* / Wyandotte, Mich.
Ellen Carlson, *St. Paul Pioneer Press Dispatch* / St. Paul, Minn.
Toni Cashnelli, *The Cincinnati Enquirer* / Cincinnati, Ohio
Libby Clark, *Los Angeles Sentinel* / Los Angeles, Calif.
Elaine Corn, *Sacramento Bee* / Sacramento, Calif.
Kitty Crider, *Austin American-Statesman* / Austin, Texas
Ann Criswell, *Houston Chronicle* / Houston, Texas
Peggy Daum, *The Milwaukee Journal* / Milwaukee, Wis.
Sue Dawson, *The Columbus Dispatch* / Columbus, Ohio
Mary Ann Dedow, *Oshkosh Northwestern* / Oshkosh, Wis.
Barb Durbin, *The Oregonian* / Portland, Ore.
Louise Durman, *The Knoxville News-Sentinel* / Knoxville, Tenn.
Clara Eschmann, *Macon Telegraph and News* / Macon, Ga.
Tui Flower, *New Zealand Newspapers Limited* / Auckland, New Zealand
Janet Beighle French, *Plain Dealer* / Cleveland, Ohio
Linda Giuca, *The Hartford Courant* / Hartford, Conn.
Barbara Goldman, *Deseret News* / Salt Lake City, Utah
Dotty Griffith, *Dallas Morning News* / Dallas, Texas
Lorrie Guttman, *Tallahassee Democrat* / Tallahassee, Fla.
Marge Hanley, *The Indianapolis News* / Indianapolis, Ind.
Charlotte Hansen, *The Jamestown Sun* / Jamestown N.D.
Karen Haram, *San Antonio Express and News* / San Antonio, Texas
Natalie Haughton, *Daily News* / Los Angeles, Calif.
Barbara Hertenstein, *St. Louis Post-Dispatch* / St. Louis, Mo.
Romaine Galey Hon, *Idaho Statesman* / Boise, Idaho
Sharon Hudgins, *The Stars and Stripes* / West Germany

Ginger Johnston, *The Oregonian* / Portland, Oregon
Sheryl Julian, *The Boston Globe* / Boston, Mass.
Margaret Kirkwood, Toorak Garden, Australia
Dolores Kostelni, Lexington, Va.
Alice Krueger, *Winnipeg Free Press* / Winnipeg, Manitoba, Canada
Faye Levy, *Bon Appetit* / Los Angeles, Calif.
Maxine Levy, Dallas, Texas
Kathy Lindsley, *Times-Union* / Rochester, N.Y.
Patricia Mack, *The News Tribune* / Woodbridge, N.J.
Louis Mahoney, *The Richmond News Leader* / Richmond, Va.
Jann Malone, *Richmond Times-Dispatch* / Richmond, Va.
Barbara McQuade, *The Vancouver Sun* / Vancouver, B.C., Canada
Marty Meitus, *Rocky Mountain News* / Denver, Colo.
Woodene Merriman, *The Pittsburgh Post-Gazette* / Pittsburgh, Pa.
Jane Milza, *Staten Island Advance* / Staten Island, N.Y.
Mary Lou Montgomery, *Hannibal Courier-Post* / Hannibal, Mo.
Donna Morgan, *The Salt Lake Tribune* / Salt Lake City, Utah
Marilyn Myers, *Arkansas Gazette* / Little Rock, Ark.
Joan Nathan, Chevy Chase, Md.
Janice Okun, *Buffalo News* / Buffalo, N.Y.
Barbara Gibbs Ostmann, *St. Louis Post-Dispatch* / St. Louis, Mo.
Eleanor Ostman, *St. Paul Pioneer Press Dispatch* / St. Paul, Minn.
Lou Pappas, *Times Tribune* / Palo Alto, Calif.
Marlene Parrish, *Pittsburgh Magazine* / Pittsburgh, Pa.
Peggy Rahn, *Pasadena Star News* / Pasadena, Calif.
Phyllis Richman, *The Washington Post* / Washington, D.C.
Peter G. Rose, *Gannett-Westchester-Rockland Newspapers* / New York
Joyce Rosencrans, *The Cincinnati Post* / Cincinnati, Ohio
Candy Sagon, *Dallas Times Herald* / Dallas, Texas
Sharon Sanders, *Chicago Sun-Times* / Chicago, Ill.
Richard Sax, New York City, N.Y.
Loretta Scott, *The Press-Enterprise* / Riverside, Calif.
Donna Segal, *The Indianapolis Star* / Indianapolis, Ind.
Louise Tennent Smith, *Columbus Ledger-Enquirer* / Columbus, Ga.
Judy Hille Walker, *The Arizona Republic* / Phoenix, Ariz.
Evelyn Wavpotich, *The Island Packet* /Hilton Head Island, S.C.
Nancy Weir, *Gwinnett Daily News* / Lawrenceville, Ga.
C. C. Williamson, *MicroScope* / Alexandria, Va.
Thayer Wine, *The Jackson Sun* / Jackson, Tenn.
Fran Zupan, *The Columbia Record* / Columbia, S.C.

Introduction

Food editors and writers love desserts. Although we try to follow a balanced and varied diet of healthful foods, there is a fascination with desserts — the pièce de résistance at any meal. Our association has published two other cookbooks, and by far the most popular category in each of those books was desserts. So this time a dessert cookbook seemed like a natural.

This book combines not only tried-and-true personal favorites, but also local and regional specialties. We've included "gourmet" treats that take some time to prepare as well as quick and easy desserts using everyday ingredients.

It appears as though apple cake is beating out other competitors for the most popular dessert in America. Almost a quarter of the contributors to this book submitted some variety of a simple-to-fix apple cake. Each contributor claimed it as a regional specialty tied to the apple harvest or a nut that is popular in the area. We selected several representative recipes as well as numerous other apple treats. Peach cobbler was the next most popular recipe, and, of course, chocolate — the favorite of dessert lovers everywhere — was the most popular ingredient in recipes.

Each recipe in the book includes a brief introduction that tells you something about the recipe, so even if you aren't in the mood for dessert, the book makes enjoyable reading.

We'd like to make it clear that these recipes are our favorites; we make no claim that they are original. When possible, we've given credit where credit is due. But in many cases, recipes just evolved or have been handed down through families, and it is difficult, if not impossible, to say from where they came.

This collection was made possible through the network of food editors represented by the Newspaper Food Editors and Writers Association, Inc. (NFEWA). This professional organization was founded in 1974 to encourage communications among food editors and writers, to fosto promote a greater understanding among other journalists. More information about NFEWA or other cookbooks is available by writing NFEWA, 520 East Main Street, Union, MO 63084.

We hope you will find these desserts as tasty as we do.

Barbara Gibbs Ostmann and Jane Baker, Co-editors

(Barbara Gibbs Ostmann is the Food Editor of the St. Louis Post-Dispatch and was president of NFEWA from 1982 to 1984. Jane Baker is the Food Editor of The Phoenix Gazette and was president of NFEWA from 1984 to 1986.)

Pies & Tarts

Bartlett Pear Pie
Blueberry Sour Cream Pie
Brown Sugar Pecan Pie
Butterscotch Apple Pie
Carmelized Apple Tart with Easy Pate
   Sucre
Chocolate Chess Pie
Fresh Apricot-Peach Pie
Grape Pie
Indiana Buttermilk Pie
Key Lime Pie
Lemon Angel Pie
Lemon Lover's Lemon Meringue Pie
Lemon Sour Cream Pie
Louisiana Black Bottom Pie
Mother's Pie Crust
Millionaire Pie
Nectarine Cream Pie
Old-Fashioned Pie Crust
Pine Barrens Blueberry Pie
Rhubarb Bavarian Cream Pie
Squash Pie
Strawberry-Apricot Tart
Sweet Potato Pie
Tarte Au Sucre (Sugar Pie)
Texas Pecan Pie
Ultimate Apple Pie
Virginia Diner Peanut Pie

Mother's Pie Crust

Jane Baker
The Phoenix Gazette, Phoenix, Ariz.

My mother and grandmother made great pies and we had homemade pies often in our family. Consequently, I learned to make pies and pie crust at an early age. My first pies were made with leftover scraps of dough and filled with brown sugar, butter and cinnamon. Today, pies are my favorite dessert to make, but I'd never consider using a store-bought crust or mix.

This is the pastry recipe my mother used, although once you get the hang of it you don't need a recipe. The "secret" is to prepare the flour and shortening mixture ahead of time and keep it in the refrigerator. Both my mother and grandmother had containers of flour mixture in the refrigerator at all times, and so do I.

For one single-crust 9-inch pie

1-1/4 cups sifted all-purpose flour
1/2 teaspoon salt
1/2 cup solid shortening
About 1/4 cup ice-cold water

For a double-crust 9-inch pie

2 cups sifted all-purpose flour
3/4 teaspoon salt
2/3 cup solid shortening
About 1/3 cup ice-cold water

In a large bowl, sift together flour and salt. Cut in shortening with pastry blender or two knives until shortening pieces are the size of small peas. For the most tender crust, cover flour mixture at this point and refrigerate 2 to 3 hours, or overnight. You can make up a lot of the flour mixture at one time and store it in the refrigerator for several months. When you are ready to make a pie, measure out a heaping cup of flour mixture for each crust; return the rest to the refrigerator.

For each crust, make a well in the center of flour-shortening mixture; add water. (If making a double-crust pie, it is better to make one crust at a time. Divide flour mixture in half and add half the water to each part.) With a fork, quickly mix to form dough into a ball. If more water is needed to make flour mixture hold together in a ball, add more water, 1 tablespoon at a time. Be careful not to add too much water.

Roll out pastry; fill and bake as indicated in the recipe.

Old-Fashioned Pie Crust

Marge Hanley
The Indianapolis News, Indianapolis, Ind.

This is my favorite pie crust recipe.

Makes enough pastry for 2 (8-inch or 9-inch) deep dish double-crust pies

4 cups unsifted all-purpose flour	1 teaspoon salt
2 tablespoons granulated sugar	1-2/3 cups lard
1-1/2 teaspoons baking powder	1 egg, slightly beaten
	1 tablespoon white vinegar
	1/2 cup ice water, divided

In a large bowl, stir together flour, sugar, baking powder and salt, mixing well. Using a pastry blender, cut in lard until mixture is crumbly and particles are about the size of small peas.

Stir together egg, vinegar and 7 tablespoons water; mix well. Pour egg mixture all at once into flour mixture and stir with a fork until it begins to clump together. Add remaining 1 tablespoon water, if needed to make dough clump.

Using hands, gently pat dough into one large ball or four small balls. Wrap in plastic wrap and refrigerate to chill, at least 2 hours, preferably overnight.

When dough is well chilled, roll out one-fourth of the dough (one small ball) on a lightly floured surface to about 1/8-inch thickness. Gently place in a deep 8-inch or 9-inch pie pan; trim around the edge to fit.

Second ball can be rolled out for a solid top crust, or rolled out and cut into 1-inch-wide strips for a lattice top. Remaining pastry can be stored several days in the refrigerator or frozen for longer storage.

Ultimate Apple Pie

Joan Nathan
Chevy Chase, Md.

Creation of the ultimate apple pie is a simple matter. There are three essential components: a good short, flaky crust; tart apples that hold their shape; and a subtle combination of sugar, spices and lemon.

There are two schools of thought on eating apple pie. To some — myself included — apple pie does not improve on standing. Others, including my husband, prefer day-old cold pie. Day-old or hot from the oven, it should be eaten with vanilla ice cream or with a wedge of Cheddar cheese.

Here is my version of the ultimate apple pie. The recipe was influenced by a recipe in "Miss Parloa's Kitchen Companion" (1887). The only difference is that the original recipe uses cloves and a pure lard crust.

Makes 6 - 8 servings

Crust

1/3 cup unsalted butter
1/3 cup lard or solid shortening
2 cups unsifted all-purpose flour
1/2 teaspoon salt
1/4 cup ice water

Filling

6 to 8 large Baldwin, Granny Smith or other hard, tart apples, peeled and cored, sliced in eighths
1/2 cup granulated sugar, or to taste
1/2 teaspoon ground cinnamon
Dash freshly grated nutmeg
1 tablespoon lemon juice, according to the tartness of apples
1/2 teaspoon grated lemon rind
1 tablespoon all-purpose flour or tapioca
2 tablespoons water
2 tablespoons unsalted butter

In a medium mixing bowl using 2 knives, cut the butter and lard or shortening into the flour and salt. When crumbly, add the water. Using the heel of your hand, press small amounts of dough away until well combined, working quickly. Form into a ball, wrap in waxed paper and refrigerate.

In a large bowl, combine apples, sugar, cinnamon, nutmeg, lemon juice, lemon rind, flour and water. Adjust the seasonings.

Roll out a little less than half the dough between two pieces of waxed paper. Turn the dough into a 9-inch pie pan, and fill with the apple mixture, which should come well above the rim of the pan. Dot with butter.

Roll out the remaining dough. Moisten the rim of the bottom crust with cold water and cover with the top crust, crimping top to bottom. With a fork, prick holes in the top.

Bake in a preheated 450-degree oven for 15 minutes, then reduce oven temperature to 350 degrees and bake 30 minutes. Serve immediately or the next day, but not the day after.

Louisiana Black Bottom Pie

Pat Baldridge
Morning Advocate/State-Times, Baton Rouge, La.

This is a glorious memory from childhood. My mother, Margaret Wilson, always made this recipe. Oh, how disappointed I was when, later in life, I tasted the more usual version.

Makes 6 - 8 servings

1 package (8-1/2 ounces) chocolate wafers, crushed or ground
1/4 cup margarine or butter, melted
1 package (16 ounces) marshmallows
1 cup milk
1 cup heavy cream, whipped
1 package (7 ounces) flaked coconut
Pinch salt

In a small bowl, combine crushed wafers and margarine; mix well. Reserve a little of this mixture to sprinkle on top of the pie. Press the remaining mixture into the bottom and up the sides of a 9-inch pie pan. Bake in a preheated 350-degree oven for 10 minutes. Remove from oven and cool.

In a large saucepan, slowly melt marshmallows in milk until well blended; cool. Fold in whipped cream and coconut. Add salt.

Fill crust with marshmallow mixture. Sprinkle with reserved crumb mixture. Chill several hours before serving.

Butterscotch Apple Pie

Claire Barriger

The Leader-Post, Regina, Saskatchewan, Canada

"Easy as pie" is a fact with this fool-proof version of an old favorite. There's a flavorful rolled oats crust, which is baked ahead of time; a buttery apple filling that is cooked on top of the stove; and a tantalizing topping that has to be tasted to be appreciated.

Makes 6 - 8 servings

Crust

2 cups quick-cooking rolled oats

1/2 teaspoon ground cinnamon

1/2 cup butter or margarine, melted

1/4 cup brown sugar

Filling

4 large cooking apples

1/4 cup water

1/4 cup light corn syrup

Apple juice

1/4 cup brown sugar

2 tablespoons cornstarch

1/2 teaspoon salt

1/2 teaspoon ground cinnamon

2 tablespoons butter or margarine

Topping

1/2 to 3/4 cup heavy cream

1/4 cup crushed peanut brittle

1/2 teaspoon finely grated orange rind

For the crust, combine oats, cinnamon, butter and brown sugar in a medium mixing bowl. Mix well. Pat into a 9-inch pie pan. Bake in a preheated 350-degree oven for 15 minutes, or until golden brown. Cool.

For the filling, peel, core and slice apples. In a large saucepan, combine apples, water and corn syrup. Cover and cook gently until apples are tender, but not mushy. Drain off liquid, measure it and add apple juice to make 2/3 cup liquid.

In another saucepan, combine the brown sugar, cornstarch, salt and cinnamon. Stir in the 2/3 cup apple liquid. Add butter. Cook until thickened, stirring constantly. Fold in cooked apple slices. Pour filling into baked and cooled pie crust. Cool before adding topping.

For the topping, whip cream until stiff. Fold in crushed peanut brittle and grated orange rind. Spread over cooled apple filling. Refrigerate pie until serving time.

Bartlett Pear Pie

Lou Pappas
Times Tribune, Palo Alto, Calif.

Pears are one of Oregon's treats. My family made this pie with pears picked from the neighbor's trees. It is delicious, expecially with whipped cream for a topping.

Makes 8 servings

Sweet crust
1/2 cup butter
1-1/3 cups all-purpose flour

1 egg

Filling
6 Bartlett pears
2 eggs
1 cup granulated sugar
2 tablespoons butter, melted
2 tablespoons heavy cream

1 teaspoon vanilla
1/2 teaspoon grated lemon peel
3 tablespoons all-purpose flour
Whipped cream, for topping

For sweet crust, cut butter into flour in a small bowl until mixture is crumbly. Mix in egg. Reserve 1/2 cup crumbs; pat remainder into bottom and sides of a 10- or 11-inch flan pan with removeable bottom.

For filling, peel and slice pears; arrange in crust-lined pan.

Beat eggs until thick and lemon colored. Beat in sugar. Add melted butter, cream, vanilla, lemon peel and flour; blend well. Pour over pears. Sprinkle with reserved 1/2 cup crumbs from the sweet crust.

Bake in a preheated 425-degree oven for 15 minutes, then reduce oven temperature to 400 degrees and continue baking 25 minutes, or until filling is set and golden brown.

Serve with whipped cream.

Caramelized Apple Tart

Toni Cashnelli

The Cincinnati Enquirer, Cincinnati, Ohio

Marilyn Harris, who has a cooking school in Cincinnati, learned to make this tart at the elbow of Georges Blanc of La Mere Blanc in Vonnas, France. As she discovered once she came home and tried to approximate the unique flavor, "Our Golden Delicious apples most closely resemble the apples we used in France."

Makes 6 - 8 servings

4 large, firm Golden Delicious apples
1 recipe Easy Pate Sucre (recipe follows)
1/2 cup unsalted butter, at room temperature, divided

1/2 cup plus 2 tablespoons granulated sugar, divided
Whipped cream lightly sweetened with sugar (optional)

Peel and core the apples. Cut apples in half and then into thin slices.

Roll out Pate Sucre dough to 1/8-inch thickness on a floured surface. Cut into an 11- to 12-inch circle. (Use a tart pan or flan ring as a pattern.) Place circle of dough on a large baking sheet. Prick with a fork. Dot dough with 2 tablespoons butter and sprinkle with 2 tablespoons sugar. Arrange the apple slices in a circular pattern on the dough. Blend remaining 6 tablespoons butter with 4 tablespoons sugar and distribute over the apples. Sprinkle with 2 tablespoons sugar.

Bake in the lower one-third of a preheated 425-degree oven for 10 minutes. Remove from oven. Sprinkle remaining 2 tablespoons sugar over the top. Return to oven and bake 10 to 15 minutes longer, or until golden.

Serve warm as is, or topped with lightly sweetened whipped cream.

Easy Pate Sucre

1-1/2 cups unbleached flour
1/4 to 1/2 teaspoon salt
2 tablespoons granulated sugar
1 egg yolk

1/2 cup cold, unsalted butter, cut into 8 pieces
About 5 tablespoons ice water

In a food processor fitted with a steel blade, place flour, salt and sugar. Blend well. Add egg yolk and cold butter. Blend until mixture resembles a very coarse meal. Add enough ice water to moisten well. Remove from processor bowl and place on a lightly floured surface. Knead together quickly and pat into a disk. Wrap in plastic wrap and chill for at least 2 hours.

Let sit at room temperature until pliable enough to roll. Use as directed in Caramelized Apple Tart recipe.

Pine Barrens Blueberry Pie

Patricia Mack
The News Tribune, Woodbridge, N.J.

I could never understand why anyone would want to do anything but eat out of hand the wonderful blueberries that come from the New Jersey Pine Barrens. They need no embellishment. But when foods are available in abundance, creative cooks can't resist finding new ways to serve them.

This recipe comes from a friend who is a former Pine Barrens resident. If she had been native born to this desolate and mysterious locale, as her husband was, she would be called a "Piney." Pineys appreciate good, simple foods and this pie preserves the best of fresh-picked blueberries in a tasty, just-cooked blueberry sauce.

Makes 6 - 8 servings

1 (9-inch) pie crust, baked
4 cups fresh blueberries, rinsed and well drained, divided
1 cup granulated sugar
3 tablespoons cornstarch
1/4 teaspoon salt
1/4 cup water mixed with 1 teaspoon lemon juice
1 tablespoon butter or margarine

Line the baked and cooled pie crust with 2 cups blueberries. In a medium saucepan, mix together sugar, cornstarch and salt. Add remaining 2 cups berries and water with lemon juice; mix well. Cook over medium heat until thickened. Remove from the heat; add butter. Cool. Pour over berries in pie crust. Chill until serving time.

Strawberry-Apricot Tart

Joyce Rosencrans
The Cincinnati Post, Cincinnati, Ohio

*This is a showstopper dessert. A butter-rich tart crust
is filled with a luscious cream cheese custard and topped
with perfect whole strawberries. I created this dessert
in honor of the first red, ripe strawberries of May — the
southern Ohio crop is always ready by Memorial Day.*

Makes 7 servings

Pastry

1-1/4 cups sifted all-purpose
flour
1/4 cup granulated sugar
1/4 teaspoon salt
6 tablespoons cold butter
1 egg yolk

1 tablespoon butter, slightly
softened
About 1/2 cup apricot
preserves, divided
1 tablespoon lemon juice

Filling

1 package (3 ounces) cream
cheese, at room temperature
1/3 cup granulated sugar
2 tablespoons cornstarch
1/8 teaspoon salt
3/4 cup light cream or
half-and-half
1 scant cup milk

2 egg yolks, slightly beaten
2 scant teaspoons orange
extract (or freshly grated
orange peel)
1 pint to 1 quart fresh
strawberries (of even size,
if possible)

To make the pastry, sift flour, sugar and salt into a medium
mixing bowl. With a pastry blender, cut in 6 tablespoons cold butter
until mixture resembles coarse cornmeal. Add egg yolk; continue
cutting motion until egg is well blended; mixture should be in the
form of fairly moist crumbs.

Sprinkle pastry mixture into a 10-inch springform pan or flan
ring set on a baking sheet. Smooth pastry over the bottom and
about an inch up the sides to an even depth. Press firmly to form
a thin crust with no breaks or cracks. Make sure the inch of standing rim is not too thin; press down from the top with your index
finger, while holding the edge of the pan, to firm and thicken the
rim.

Bake pastry in a preheated 350-degree oven for 20 minutes, or until light brown around the edges. Cool on a wire rack; do not remove the pan sides yet.

When the crust is completely cool, spread it with the 1 tablespoon softened butter to prevent sogginess. On top of the butter, spread a thin layer of apricot preserves, using several tablespoons (chop any large pieces of fruit). Chill crust while making the cream filling.

To make the filling, combine cream cheese, sugar, cornstarch and salt in a medium saucepan. Place on low heat and stir until sugar is almost dissolved in cream cheese. Combine cream, milk and egg yolks; gradually stir into cream cheese mixture, which is now quite warm. Stir to keep the mixture smooth. When all of the liquid has been added, bring to boiling and let mixture bubble about 1 minute, stirring constantly.

Remove from heat; add orange extract. Set pan in ice water and keep stirring mixture to hasten cooling. Cover with waxed paper and refrigerate until completely cool.

Meanwhile, remove caps from clean, dry strawberries and leave whole unless very large.

Spread the cooled cream cheese filling over the apricot preserves in the pastry shell. Top with whole strawberries, pointed ends up, or arrange cut berries over the tart in an attractive design. Cover the entire surface, if you have enough berries.

Gently heat the remaining apricot preserves with lemon juice. When soft enough, carefully brush preserves over the strawberries to glaze.

Chill tart until serving time, leaving the sides of the pan in place until the last minute.

Fresh Apricot-Peach Pie

Barbara Goldman
Deseret News, Salt Lake City, Utah

Fruit trees, including peach and apricot trees, are commonly planted in Utah backyards. Although this pie could be made with either fruit, the unusual combination of peaches and apricots is especially nice. It's excellent served with vanilla ice cream.

Makes 6 - 8 servings

Pastry for a 9-inch double-crust pie
1-1/2 cups peeled fresh apricot halves
1-1/2 cups peeled and sliced fresh peaches
1 teaspoon lemon juice
1 cup granulated sugar
1/4 cup all-purpose flour
1/4 teaspoon ground cinnamon
2 tablespoons butter or margarine

Roll out half the pastry and fit it into a 9-inch pie pan.

In a large mixing bowl, combine apricot halves, peach slices and lemon juice. In another bowl, combine sugar, flour and cinnamon. Combine sugar mixture with fruit mixture. Turn into pastry-lined pan; dot with butter.

Roll out remaining pastry; arrange top crust over fruit. Seal and flute edges. Cut slits in top crust. Cover edge with a strip of foil to prevent excessive browning; remove foil during last 15 minutes of baking. Bake in a preheated 425-degree oven 35 to 45 minutes, or until crust is golden brown and juices begin to bubble through slits in crust.

Grape Pie

Kathy Lindsley
Times-Union, Rochester, N.Y.

This recipe comes from Naples, N.Y., a charming village in the state's Finger Lakes region. Many of the local women sell the pies at roadside stands, especially during the fall harvest time when thousands of tourists make the pilgrimage to see the foliage.

Makes 6 - 8 servings

3 cups Concord grapes
1/2 to 1 cup granulated sugar,
   to taste
3 tablespoons all-purpose flour

1 tablespoon lemon juice
1 tablespoon butter, melted
Pastry for a 9-inch double-crust
   pie

Wash and stem grapes. Remove skins by squeezing gently; reserve skins. Heat the grape pulp to the boiling point, stirring occasionally; reduce heat and simmer 5 minutes, stirring, or until the seeds can be easily removed by pressing the pulp through a sieve. Discard the seeds. Mix reserved skins with strained pulp. Combine sugar and flour; add to grapes along with lemon juice and butter.

Pour mixture into unbaked pie crust. Position the top crust and seal edges. Make slits in top crust.

Bake in a preheated 425-degree oven for 10 minutes, then reduce oven temperature to 350 degrees and bake for 30 minutes, or until pastry browns and filling bubbles.

Note: Unbaked pie can be frozen.

Key Lime Pie

Louise Tennent Smith
Columbus Ledger-Enquirer, Columbus, Ga.

*This is the true recipe for Key lime pie. It is made
in a pastry crust, never a graham cracker crumb crust;
it is never colored a sickly green; and it is topped with
a cloud of meringue, never whipped cream. This recipe
came from Fern Butter of the Fern Inn in Islamorada,
Fla. You have to follow the recipe exactly.*

Makes 6 - 8 servings

1 can (14 ounces) sweetened
condensed milk (not
evaporated milk)
6 eggs, separated
1/2 cup lime juice (see note)

1 deep-dish 9-inch pie crust,
baked (or two 8-inch crusts)
1 tablespoon cream of tartar
1 cup granulated sugar

In a large mixing bowl with an electric mixer, beat sweetened
condensed milk and egg yolks until light and creamy (about
8 minutes). Add lime juice; let bowl rotate on low speed of mixer
for 1 second. Fold mixture a few times with a rubber spatula to
be sure juice is thoroughly blended. Pour mixture into baked pie
crust. Let stand.

With electric mixer, beat egg whites with cream of tartar for
5 minutes. Add sugar; beat 5 minutes more. Cover pie with
meringue, being sure to seal meringue to edge of crust.

Bake in a preheated 350-degree oven for about 10 minutes,
or until meringue is golden brown.

Note: Use real Key lime juice, if available.

Lemon Lover's Lemon Meringue Pie

Marie Bianco
Newsday, Long Island, N.Y.

California can thank the Gold Rush of 1849 for its lemon industry. The influx of gold prospectors increased the population tenfold and food became scarce. Undernourished miners, threatened by scurvy, were willing to pay a dollar a piece for lemons. Just think how much they would have paid for this pie!

Makes 6 - 8 servings

1 cup granulated sugar, divided
1/4 cup cornstarch, sifted
Dash salt
1 cup water
1 cup fresh lemon juice
3 egg yolks, beaten
1/4 cup butter, cut in small
   pieces

1 tablespoon grated lemon rind
1 (9-inch) pie crust, baked and
   cooled
8 egg whites, at room
   temperature
1/2 teaspoon cream of tartar,
   sifted

In the top of a double boiler, combine 3/4 cup sugar, cornstarch and salt. Gradually add water and lemon juice; whisk until smooth. Cook, stirring constantly, over boiling water until mixture thickens, about 10 minutes. Remove 1/2 cup of the lemon mixture and whisk egg yolks into it. Return this mixture to the pan along with butter and lemon rind. Stir to combine. Pour hot filling into crust.

In a large mixing bowl with an electric mixer, beat egg whites until frothy. Add cream of tartar. Beat until egg whites are stiff but not dry, gradually beating in remaining 1/4 cup sugar. Peaks should lean over slightly when beaters are lifted.

Spread meringue over hot filling, sealing it at the edge. Bake in a preheated 325-degree oven for 15 minutes, or until meringue is lightly browned.

Lemon Sour Cream Pie

Karen Haram

San Antonio Express and News, San Antonio, Texas

This pie is sinfully rich, but well worth every one of its many calories.

My mother brought this recipe home from a church potluck dinner more than 20 years ago. Its origins couldn't be more appropriate, for it is truly a heavenly recipe.

Makes 6 - 8 servings

1 cup plus 6 tablespoons granulated sugar, divided
3 tablespoons cornstarch
Dash salt
1 cup milk
3 eggs, separated
4 tablespoons butter

1 teaspoon shredded lemon peel
1/4 cup lemon juice
1 cup dairy sour cream
1 (9-inch) pie crust, baked
1/4 teaspoon cream of tartar
1/2 teaspoon vanilla

Combine 1 cup sugar with cornstarch and salt, stirring thoroughly. Slowly stir in milk, then cook and stir over medium heat until mixture is boiling and thickened.

Remove pan from heat. Blend a small amount of hot mixture into the slightly beaten egg yolks. Return egg yolk mixture to hot mixture in pan; cook and stir 2 minutes over medium heat. Add butter, lemon peel and lemon juice. Cover and cool. Fold in sour cream. Spoon mixture into baked pie crust.

Beat egg whites with cream of tartar and vanilla until soft peaks form. Gradually add remaining 6 tablespoons sugar, beating until stiff peaks form.

Top pie with the meringue, being sure to seal edges. Bake in a preheated 350-degree oven for 12 to 15 minutes, or until meringue is lightly browned.

Lemon Angel Pie

Janice Okun
Buffalo News, Buffalo, N.Y.

*This light and elegant pie is a 50-year-old recipe that
is a favorite at bridal showers in Buffalo.*

Makes 8 servings

4 egg whites
1 cup granulated sugar, divided

Lemon custard filling
4 egg yolks
1/2 cup granulated sugar
4 tablespoons fresh lemon juice

3/4 teaspoon fresh lemon juice
1 cup heavy cream

2 tablespoons grated lemon rind

In a mixing bowl with an electric mixer, beat egg whites until stiff. Gradually beat in half the sugar. Add the rest of the sugar a little at a time alternately with the lemon juice. Beat until egg whites are very stiff and glossy.

Spread meringue on the bottom and up the sides of a paper-lined 9-inch round layer pan. Bake in a preheated 275-degree oven for 60 minutes. Cool slightly. Remove from pan and cool completely on a wire rack.

Meanwhile, prepare lemon custard filling. In a medium mixing bowl with an electric mixer, beat egg yolks until thick and lemon colored. Gradually beat in the sugar, then blend in lemon juice and lemon rind. Pour lemon mixture into the top of a double boiler. Cook over hot water, stirring constantly, until mixture is thick, 5 to 8 minutes. Cool.

After filling has cooled, whip the cream in a medium bowl with an electric mixer until stiff.

Spread half of the whipped cream in bottom of the cooled meringue shell. Spread with cooled lemon custard filling, then top with remaining whipped cream. Chill about 12 hours before serving.

Nectarine Cream Pie

Bev Bennett
Chicago Sun-Times, Chicago, Ill.

This pie is outstanding. Be sure to use good, sweet-tart nectarines. It also can be prepared with peaches.

Makes 6 - 8 servings

Pastry for a 9-inch single-crust pie
1 egg beaten with 1 tablespoon water, for egg wash
6 to 7 ripe, medium nectarines, pitted and sliced to yield 4 cups

3/4 cup granulated sugar
2 tablespoons all-purpose flour
1 egg
1 egg yolk
3/4 cup heavy cream

Prepare pastry according to your favorite recipe. Roll out and fit into a 9-inch pie plate. Line pastry with parchment paper and fill with pie weights. Cover edges of crust with foil. Bake in a preheated 400-degree oven for 10 minutes. Remove from the oven and remove weights, but keep foil on edges of crust. Return to the oven for about 8 minutes, or until lightly browned. Brush baked crust with egg wash.

Toss nectarines with sugar and flour. Spoon into pie crust. Beat together egg and egg yolk; whisk into cream. Pour mixture over nectarines in crust.

Bake in a preheated 425-degree oven for 10 minutes. Reduce oven temperature to 350 degrees and bake for 35 to 40 minutes, or until pastry is golden and filling is fairly firm.

Remove pie from oven and cool. Serve warm or at room temperature. This pie tastes best when served the day it is made.

Rhubarb Bavarian Cream Pie

Claire Barriger
The Leader-Post, Regina, Saskatchewan, Canada

Rhubarb was always a sure sign of spring — until home freezers made it a treat we could enjoy all year round. Even if you don't have a home freezer, packages of frozen rhubarb are available in supermarkets. I made up this recipe to celebrate Valentine's Day several years ago. If desired, you can make it in a heart-shaped pan.

Makes 6 - 8 servings

2 cups sliced rhubarb
1/2 cup plus 2 tablespoons
  honey, divided
1/4 cup water

1 tablespoon unflavored
  gelatin softened in
  2 tablespoons cold water
3/4 cup heavy cream
Red food coloring (optional)
1 (9-inch) pie crust, baked

In a medium saucepan, combine rhubarb, 1/2 cup honey and water. Cook until rhubarb is soft. Measure while hot; if necessary, add hot water to make 2 cups fruit mixture. Stir softened gelatin mixture into hot rhubarb. Chill until partly set, but not firm.

In a large mixing bowl, whip cream until stiff peaks form. Gradually blend in the remaining 2 tablespoons honey. Fold in partly set rhubarb mixture. Add a few drops of red food coloring, if desired.

Pour filling into pie crust. Chill until firm.

Indiana Buttermilk Pie

Marge Hanley
The Indianapolis News, Indianapolis, Ind.

Buttermilk pie is a specialty of Indiana. Its ancestry can be traced to the transparent and chess pies of the South, which had their genesis in England. This pie is not for the calorie conscious, because one piece contains more than 500 calories. But is it good!

Similar to a custard pie, this version contains eggs, and the filling is added to the unbaked pie crust.

Makes 6 - 8 servings

1/2 cup butter, at room
   temperature
2 cups granulated sugar
3 eggs
2 tablespoons all-purpose flour

1 cup buttermilk
1 teaspoon vanilla
1 (9-inch) pie crust, unbaked
Freshly grated nutmeg
   (optional)

Have all the ingredients at room temperature. Put oven rack in the lower third of the oven.

In a mixer bowl, beat butter until creamy. Gradually beat in sugar; beat until light and fluffy.

In a separate bowl, slightly beat eggs. Mix in flour, buttermilk and vanilla. Add egg mixture to butter mixture; beat on high speed of electric mixer until well combined and mixture looks slightly curdled.

Slowly pour mixture into unbaked pie crust. Sprinkle lightly with nutmeg, if desired.

Carefully place pie on bottom rack of a preheated 325-degree oven and bake about 55 minutes, or until a knife comes out clean when inserted in the center. The top should be light golden brown.

Partly cool pie on a wire rack, then refrigerate for about an hour before cutting to serve. Store in the refrigerator.

Chocolate Chess Pie

Louise Durman
The Knoxville News-Sentinel, Knoxville, Tenn.

Chess Pie is a Tennessee favorite. Here is a new version that has become popular with chocoholics.

Makes 6 - 8 servings

1-1/2 cups granulated sugar
3 tablespoons cocoa powder
1/4 cup butter, melted
2 eggs

1 can (5.3 ounces) evaporated milk (2/3 cup)
1 teaspoon vanilla
1/8 teaspoon salt
1 (9-inch) pie crust, unbaked

In a medium mixing bowl, combine sugar and cocoa. Add butter, eggs, evaporated milk, vanilla and salt. Mix well. Pour into unbaked pie crust. Bake in a preheated 350-degree oven for 35 to 40 minutes, or until knife inserted near center comes out clean.

Brown Sugar Pecan Pie

Clara Eschmann
Macon Telegraph and News, Macon, Ga.

Georgia is noted for its delicious pecans. This recipe is a little different than the traditional ones made with corn syrup.

Makes 6 - 8 servings

2 cups firmly packed light brown sugar
6 tablespoons butter or margarine

2 eggs
1 cup broken pecans
1 (9-inch) pie crust, unbaked

In a large mixing bowl, cream brown sugar and butter. Add eggs; mix well. Add pecans. Pour mixture into unbaked pie crust. Bake in a preheated 350-degree oven for 1 hour, or until knife inserted near center comes out clean.

Texas Pecan Pie
Kitty Crider
Austin American-Statesman, Austin, Texas

Texans, known for their individualism, have their own ideas about pecan pies. This version of the classic recipe was given to me by a reader of the food section, Elsie East, and it is one of our most-requested Thanksgiving recipes. The secret ingredient is a hint of cinnamon.

Makes 8 servings

1 cup light corn syrup
1/2 cup granulated sugar
3 tablespoons all-purpose flour
1/2 teaspoon salt
1/2 teaspoon (scant) ground cinnamon

1/2 teaspoon vanilla
2 eggs
1 cup broken pecans
3 tablespoons butter, melted
1 (9-inch) pie crust, unbaked

In a large mixing bowl, combine corn syrup, sugar, flour, salt, cinnamon, vanilla, eggs, pecans and melted butter. Pour into unbaked pie crust.

Bake on the low rack of a preheated 300-degree oven for 1 hour, or until knife inserted near center comes out clean.

Virginia Diner Peanut Pie
Louis Mahoney
The Richmond News Leader, Richmond, Va.

Wakefield, Va., is in the heart of peanut country, and the Virginia Diner is in Wakefield, so naturally peanuts are on the menu.

Owner Bill Galloway tells about making this pie: "First you put the peanuts in a white ham sack and beat them well with a wooden mallet. If you don't put them in the cloth bag, they'll just fly all over the kitchen." He says beating the peanuts in a ham bag also adds flavor. If you don't have a ham bag (from a country ham) handy, crush the peanuts in a plastic bag or between sheets of waxed paper.

2 eggs
1/3 cup butter, melted
1-1/2 cups granulated sugar
1 cup light corn syrup

2 tablespoons all-purpose flour
1/2 pound salted Virginia
  peanuts, crushed
1 (9-inch) pie crust, unbaked

In a medium bowl, beat eggs. Add melted butter, sugar, corn syrup and flour; mix well. Stir in peanuts until well mixed.

Pour into unbaked pie crust. Bake in a preheated 375-degree oven 40 to 50 minutes, or until knife inserted in center comes out clean. (Filling will swell, brown and then settle.) Cool completely before slicing.

Squash Pie

Lorrie Guttman
Tallahassee Democrat, Tallahassee, Fla.

This is my all-time favorite from our bi-monthly Capital Chef recipe contest. This pie tastes like coconut custard.

Makes 6 - 8 servings

2 cups freshly grated, peeled
  yellow squash
1-1/2 cups granulated sugar
1 teaspoon cornstarch
1 teaspoon vanilla
1 teaspoon coconut extract

1 tablespoon all-purpose flour
3 eggs
1/4 cup margarine, melted
Pinch salt
1 deep-dish 9-inch pie crust,
  unbaked

In a large bowl, combine squash, sugar, cornstarch, vanilla, coconut extract, flour, eggs, margarine and salt. Mix well. Pour into unbaked pie crust.

Bake in a preheated 400-degree oven for 10 to 15 minutes; reduce oven temperature to 350 degrees and continue baking 40 to 50 minutes, or until golden brown. Shield the pie with aluminum foil if the top is browned but the center is not cooked through.

Sweet Potato Pie

Libby Clark
Los Angeles Sentinel, Los Angeles, Calif.

This is a southern classic that comes from my mother,
Emily White. It is even more tasty than pumpkin pie.

Makes 6 - 8 servings

1 (9-inch) pie crust, unbaked
1 egg beaten with 1 tablespoon water, for egg wash
3 large sweet potatoes, peeled, cooked, well drained and mashed
1 cup granulated sugar
1/2 cup butter, softened
1/2 teaspoon salt
1 teaspoon ground cinnamon
1 teaspoon ground nutmeg
1 teaspoon ground allspice
1 cup milk
4 eggs, slightly beaten
1 teaspoon vanilla

Prepare 9-inch pie crust and put in the freezer for 30 minutes. Brush crust with egg wash.

In a large bowl, combine cooked sweet potatoes, sugar, butter, salt, cinnamon, nutmeg and allspice. Mix well. In another bowl, combine milk, eggs and vanilla; combine thoroughly. Pour milk mixture into sweet potato mixture; stir to combine. Pour mixture into unbaked pie crust.

Bake in a preheated 375-degree oven for 45 to 50 minutes, or until knife inserted in center comes out clean.

Blueberry Sour Cream Pie

Claire Barriger
The Leader-Post, Regina, Saskatchewan, Canada

A friend brought a recipe for blueberry cheesecake
back from her vacation in Nova Scotia. I halved the fill-
ing recipe and made this simple-to-prepare pie.

Makes 6 servings

2 cups fresh or frozen blueberries
1 (8- or 9-inch) ready-to-serve cookie crumb crust or regular pie crust (your favorite recipe or store-bought)
1 cup dairy sour cream
1/4 cup granulated sugar
1 egg yolk
1/2 teaspoon vanilla
Whipped cream and additional blueberries, for garnish (optional)

Spread blueberries in crust. In a small bowl, combine sour cream, sugar, egg yolk and vanilla; pour over blueberries.

Bake in a preheated 375-degree oven for 45 minutes, or until set and lightly browned at edges. Chill.

Serve as is or garnish with whipped cream and a few blueberries.

Note: Leftover pie can be frozen for later enjoyment.

Millionaire Pie

Charlotte Hansen
The Jamestown Sun, Jamestown, N.D.

*This was one of my mother-in-law's favorite recipes, and
I often use it for a handy summer dessert.*

Makes 2 pies, 8 servings each

2 (9-inch) graham cracker crusts (your favorite recipe or store-bought)
1 egg yolk, beaten
1 can (14 ounces) sweetened condensed milk (not evaporated milk)
1/3 cup lemon juice
2 cans (20 ounces each) crushed pineapple, well drained

1 carton (20 ounces) frozen non-dairy whipped topping, thawed
1 cup coarsely chopped walnuts
1 jar (10 ounces) maraschino cherries, drained and halved

Coat graham cracker crusts with beaten egg yolk. Bake in a preheated 325-degree oven for 5 minutes; cool.

In a large mixing bowl, combine sweetened condensed milk and lemon juice; mix well. Add well-drained pineapple, whipped topping, walnuts and all but 16 cherry halves. Mix well. Divide mixture between the two prepared crusts. Refrigerate overnight.

Just before serving, decorate each pie with 8 cherry halves.

Tarte Au Sucre
(Sugar Pie)

Julian Armstrong
The Gazette, Montreal, Quebec, Canada

*Quebec's best-known dessert, sugar pie, is often
made with brown sugar instead of the original maple
syrup or maple sugar. These spring treats have become
scarce and expensive because of the devastation
suffered by Canada's sugar maple trees from acid rain.*

*This recipe is the best sugar pie I've ever tasted. It
comes from the personal files of Madame Jehane
Benoit, French Canada's leading culinary authority and
cookbook author, who died in November, 1987, at the
age of 83. She learned how to make this recipe from
her "grand-mere."*

Makes 6 - 8 servings

Pastry for a 9-inch single-crust
  pie
1-1/2 cups maple syrup
1/2 teaspoon baking soda
1/4 teaspoon vanilla

1 cup all-purpose flour
1 cup dark brown sugar
Pinch ground nutmeg
1/3 cup butter, chilled

Line 9-inch pie pan with pastry, crimping edge.

Measure syrup into a mixing bowl. Stir in baking soda and vanilla. Pour mixture into pastry.

Mix flour, sugar and nutmeg in a bowl, then cut in butter with a pastry blender or two knives. Spread flour mixture over syrup mixture in pastry.

Set pie pan on a cookie sheet with sides or on aluminum foil, because filling might bubble over during baking. Bake in a preheated 350-degree oven for 30 minutes. Cool. Pie is best served cold, but not chilled.

Cakes & Tortes

Almond Torte with Apricot Butter Cream
Apfel Kuchen
Apple Torte
Applesauce Cake
Banana Split Cake
Bite-Size Cupcakes
Black Bottom Cups
Blueberry Cheesecake
Blueberry Pecan Family Cake
Chocolate Orange Torte
Chocolate Walnut Torte
Clove Cake
Cornmeal Pound Cake
Danish Strawberry Cake
Dark Orange Cake with Orange Frosting
Devil's Food Cake with Chocolate Cream
    Cheese Frosting
Fresh Ginger Cake
Fudge Cake with Chocolate Frosting
Gateau Sirop (Syrup Cake)
Grandmother's Boiled Raisin Cake
Hawaiian Wedding Cake
Heath Bar Mocha Cheesecake
Italian Cheesecake
Mexican Chocolate Cake with Mexican
    Chocolate Icing
Mocha Pound Cake
Mrs. 'Iggins Icing
Never-Fail Passover Sponge Cake
North Georgia Apple Cake
Oatmeal Cake with Frosting
Plum Coffee Cake
Poppy Seed Cake
Pumpkin Cheesecake with Cranberry
    Sauce
Raspberry Brownie Torte
Schaum Torte (German Meringue Torte)
Sour Cream Pound Cake
Southern Caramel Cake with Caramel
    Frosting
Swedish Nut Cake with Caramel Frosting
Texas Carrot Cake with Icing
Triple Threat Chocolate Cake, Brownies
    or Truffles
Walnut Wonder Coffee Cake

Applesauce Cake

Donna Segal
The Indianapolis Star, Indianapolis, Ind.

This home-style dessert has been a family favorite for years.

Makes 16 - 20 servings

2-1/2 cups all-purpose flour
2 teaspoons baking soda
2 teaspoons ground cloves
2 teaspoons ground cinnamon
Dash salt
1 cup coarsely chopped pecans

1 cup unsalted margarine, softened
2 scant cups granulated sugar
2 eggs, at room temperature
1 can (16 ounces) applesauce, at room temperature

Topping
3 tablespoons margarine
1/2 cup firmly packed brown sugar

3 tablespoons milk, cream or non-dairy liquid creamer

Sift together flour, baking soda, cloves, cinnamon and salt. Dredge pecans with 1 cup flour mixture; set aside flour and flour-pecan mixtures.

In the large mixing bowl of an electric mixer, cream margarine and sugar; add eggs, one at a time, beating well after each addition until incorporated.

Alternately add flour mixture and applesauce to creamed mixture, beginning with flour and ending with flour-pecan mixture. Do not overmix.

Spoon batter into a greased and floured 9-inch tube pan or two 8x4x3-inch loaf pans. Bake in a preheated 375-degree oven for 45 to 60 minutes, or until a wooden pick inserted in the center comes out clean. Do not overbake.

Meanwhile, prepare topping. Melt margarine in a small saucepan. Add brown sugar and milk. Cook over medium heat until mixture boils. Turn off heat and let mixture stand until ready to spoon on cake. (Mixture will caramelize on cake.)

When cake is done, spoon topping over the top and return cake to the oven until the topping bubbles, about 5 minutes. Remove from the oven and cool on a rack.

Note: This cake freezes well.

North Georgia Apple Cake

Anne Byrn

Atlanta Journal-Constitution, Atlanta, Ga.

There's no better use for the tasty apples of northern Georgia than this cake.

Makes 15 - 18 servings

1-1/2 cups vegetable oil
1-1/2 cups granulated sugar
1/2 cup light brown sugar
3 eggs
3 cups all-purpose flour
1 teaspoon baking soda
2 teaspoons ground cinnamon

1/2 teaspoon ground nutmeg
1/2 teaspoon salt
3-1/2 cups peeled and chopped
   tart fresh apples
1 cup chopped walnuts
2 teaspoons vanilla

Glaze
3 tablespoons butter
3 tablespoons light brown sugar
3 tablespoons granulated sugar

3 tablespoons heavy cream
1/4 teaspoon vanilla

In a large mixing bowl, combine oil, granulated sugar and brown sugar; blend well. Add eggs, one at a time, beating well after each addition.

Sift together flour, baking soda, cinnamon, nutmeg and salt. Add to egg mixture and blend well. Add apples, nuts and vanilla; mix in with a spoon.

Pour batter into a buttered and floured 10-inch tube pan. Bake in a preheated 325-degree oven for 1-1/4 hours, or until cake tests done.

Remove from oven and let rest in the pan 20 minutes.

While cake is resting, prepare glaze. Combine butter, brown sugar, granulated sugar, cream and vanilla in a small saucepan; bring to a boil and continue boiling 1 minute. Remove from heat.

Remove cake from pan and put on a wire rack or platter. Spoon glaze over warm cake. Serve warm.

Apfel Kuchen

Peggy Daum

The Milwaukee Journal, Milwaukee, Wis.

In Milwaukee, tortes are fancy desserts for company. Kuchens are what you bake for the family. And Apfel Kuchen has to be one of the most popular.

At least half a dozen cooks that were featured in The Milwaukee Journal's series that is called "Best Cook on the Block" offered a recipe similar to this as a family favorite. Some used this name; others called it Dutch apple cake. Toppings varied somewhat, but all featured a short-dough crust filled with apple slices.

Marie Pitting of Milwaukee's West Side can claim seniority, so this is her version. It also is included in Volume II of "The Best Cook on the Block Cookbook."

Makes 12 - 16 servings

Streusel topping
3/4 cup granulated sugar
2 tablespoons all-purpose flour

1/4 teaspoon ground cinnamon
2 tablespoons butter

Kuchen
1-1/4 cups all purpose flour
3 tablespoons granulated sugar
1/2 teaspoon salt
1 teaspoon baking powder
1/2 cup butter, cut in chunks
1 egg yolk

2 tablespoons milk
5 to 6 McIntosh or Cortland apples
2 tablespoons whipping cream, half-and-half or milk

For the streusel topping, combine sugar, flour, cinnamon and butter. Mix ingredients with fingertips until mixture resembles coarse crumbs; set aside.

To prepare the kuchen, combine flour, sugar, salt and baking powder in a large mixing bowl. Stir to blend. Cut in butter with a pastry blender, 2 knives or fingertips until mixture resembles coarse crumbs.

In a small bowl, mix together egg yolk and milk. Add to flour mixture, stirring to form soft dough. Press dough into and slightly up the sides of an ungreased 13x9x2-inch baking pan.

Peel and core apples. Cut into thin slices. Arrange slices in neat rows atop dough. Sprinkle apples with streusel topping. Drizzle cream over topping.

Bake in a 350-degree oven 1 hour, or until browned. Remove from oven and cover immediately with waxed paper to keep apples soft. Serve warm or cooled. Cut into squares or rectangles to serve.

Blueberry Pecan Family Cake

Harriett Aldridge
Arkansas Gazette, Little Rock, Ark.

I picked up this recipe from a sheet of recipes provided by a blueberry grower in North Arkansas to those who purchased berries. However, as do many cooks, I have made a few changes. It is a delicious, easy-to-make cake.

Makes 8 servings

1 cup granulated sugar	1/2 cup whole wheat flour
1 teaspoon ground cinnamon	1 teaspoon baking soda
1 egg	1/2 teaspoon salt
2/3 cup vegetable oil	1-1/2 cups blueberries, rinsed
1/4 cup water	and drained
1 teaspoon vanilla	1 cup chopped pecans
1 cup all-purpose flour	

In a large mixing bowl, combine sugar and cinnamon, then add egg, oil, water and vanilla. Combine all-purpose flour, whole wheat flour, baking soda and salt. Stir flour mixture into sugar mixture. Stir in blueberries and nuts.

Pour batter into a greased 8-inch square baking pan. Bake in a preheated 350-degree oven for 35 to 45 minutes, or until done.

Note: This cake can be frozen, but it will not be quite as good as fresh. Thaw frozen cake unwrapped, or it will become damp and gooey.

Swedish Nut Cake

Lou Pappas
Times Tribune, Palo Alto, Calif.

This was a favorite childhood cake that Mom would whip up before dinner. Sometimes we called it Lazy Daisy Cake. We all loved the frosting.

Makes 15 - 18 servings

3/4 cup milk
3 tablespoons butter
5 eggs
1-1/2 cups granulated sugar
1-1/2 teaspoons vanilla
1-1/2 cups all-purpose flour

1-1/2 teaspoons baking
   powder
1/2 teaspoon salt
Caramel Frosting
   (recipe follows)

In a small saucepan, heat milk and butter until the butter melts; set aside.

With an electric mixer, beat eggs until thick and lemon colored. Beat in sugar and vanilla, mixing well.

Sift together flour, baking powder and salt. Add flour mixture to egg mixture; mix well. Gently stir in hot milk mixture.

Pour batter into buttered and floured 13x9x2-inch baking pan. Bake in a preheated 350-degree oven for 30 minutes, or until top springs back when touched lightly.

Spread top with Caramel Frosting and place under the broiler until bubbly, about 1 minute. Let cool, then cut into squares.

Caramel Frosting

4 tablespoons butter
3 tablespoons heavy cream
1 cup firmly packed brown
   sugar

3/4 cup chopped walnuts or
   pecans or shredded coconut

In a saucepan, combine butter, cream and brown sugar. Heat, stirring constantly, until mixture bubbles. Stir in nuts or coconut. Use as directed with Swedish Nut Cake.

Walnut Wonder Coffee Cake

Joyce Rosencrans
The Cincinnati Post, Cincinnati, Ohio

Ohio's Amish population is centered in Holmes County, northeast of Columbus. The Amish are good dairymen, producing prodigious quantities of mild Swiss cheese and sweet butter. This butter coffee cake recipe was the prize of a weekend drive through Amish country; it was shared by an Amish farm woman who puts up 900 jars of fruit preserves and jelly every summer.

Makes 15 servings

1 cup butter
1 cup granulated sugar
2 eggs
1 teaspoon vanilla
1 cup dairy sour cream

2 cups all-purpose flour
1 teaspoon baking powder
1 teaspoon baking soda
1/2 teaspoon salt

Filling
1/3 cup packed brown sugar
1/4 cup granulated sugar

1 teaspoon ground cinnamon
1 cup finely chopped walnuts

In a large bowl, cream butter and sugar until light and fluffy. Stir in eggs and vanilla. Add sour cream.

Sift together flour, baking powder, baking soda and salt. Gradually add flour mixture to butter mixture.

In a separate bowl, mix the brown sugar, granulated sugar, cinnamon and walnuts for the filling.

Spread half the batter in a greased 13x9x2-inch baking pan. Sprinkle with half the filling mixture. Spoon on the remaining batter, spreading it carefully to cover the filling. Sprinkle remaining filling over top of batter. Bake in a preheated 350-degree oven for 35 minutes, or until done.

Southern Caramel Cake

Louise Tennent Smith
Columbus Ledger-Enquirer, Columbus, Ga.

I heard about a woman just across the Chattahoochee River in Phenix City, Ala., who had won 19 blue ribbons for her cake baking. After a lot of persuasion, the woman, Patricia Crow McElwee, gave me the recipe for her caramel cake — the only one she makes that she says she could sit right down and eat all by herself. So could I.

Makes 12 - 15 servings

1 cup butter or margarine
2 cups granulated sugar
4 eggs
1 teaspoon vanilla
2-1/4 cups all-purpose flour

1/2 teaspoon baking soda
1/2 teaspoon baking powder
1/4 teaspoon salt
1 cup buttermilk
Caramel Frosting (recipe follows)

In a large mixing bowl, cream butter and sugar. Beat in eggs and vanilla. Sift together flour, baking soda, baking powder and salt. Add flour mixture alternately with buttermilk to egg mixture.

Pour batter into 3 greased and floured 9-inch cake pans. Bake in a preheated 350-degree oven for 25 to 30 minutes, or until done.

Cool cakes slightly, then remove from pans. Cool on wire racks. Fill and frost with Caramel Frosting.

Caramel Frosting

Makes enough frosting for a 3-layer cake

4 cups granulated sugar, divided
1 cup milk

1 cup butter or margarine
2 teaspoons vinegar
1 teaspoon baking soda

In a large saucepan, combine 3-1/2 cups sugar, milk and butter. Bring to a rapid boil; remove from heat.

In a small saucepan, heat remaining 1/2 cup sugar over low heat until it caramelizes. (Stir the sugar as it starts to melt and continue stirring until all the sugar is melted and it turns a golden brown color.) Carefully add hot sugar mixture to milk mixture in large saucepan.

Return milk mixture to medium heat; cook to the hard ball stage (250 degrees on a candy thermometer). Remove from heat and add vinegar and baking soda. Cool for a few minutes, then beat until of spreading consistency.

Use to fill and frost Southern Caramel Cake.

Gateau Sirop
(Syrup Cake)

Pat Baldridge
Morning Advocate/State-Times, Baton Rouge, La.

This is a handy, everyday cake that is often made in southern Louisiana. Pure cane syrup is a popular Louisiana product. Light molasses can be substituted for the cane syrup, if it is not available.

Makes 12 - 15 servings

1-1/2 cups granulated sugar
1 scant cup vegetable oil
1 cup pure cane syrup
2 teaspoons baking soda
   dissolved in 1 cup boiling
   water
1 teaspoon ground ginger

1/2 teaspoon ground cloves
1/2 teaspoon ground cinnamon
2-1/2 cups all-purpose flour,
   sifted
Pinch salt
2 eggs, well beaten

In a large mixing bowl, combine sugar, vegetable oil, cane syrup, baking soda dissolved in boiling water, ginger, cloves, cinnamon, flour and salt. Add eggs. Do not overmix.

Pour batter into a greased 13x9x2-inch baking pan. Bake in a preheated 350-degree oven for 35 to 40 minutes, or until cake springs back when touched.

Fudge Cake

Fran Zupan
The Columbia Record, Columbia, S.C.

I really can't say that Fudge Cake is a regional cake, except that Southern people like it — but so do people in other parts of the country! Fudge Cake is usually made for Christmas, birthdays or as a special ending to a nice dinner. It is also nice to have instead of the fruitcakes generally served at Christmas.

Fudge Cake can be prepared ahead of time, before the filling and frosting are added. Bake the layers, then store them in the freezer in airtight containers. The cook can prepare the filling and frosting when needed, and assemble the cake then.

Makes 20 servings

3 cups sifted cake flour
  (see note)
1-1/2 teaspoons baking soda
2 teaspoons baking powder
3/4 teaspoon salt
3/4 cup butter
2-1/4 cups granulated sugar
1-1/2 teaspoons vanilla

3 eggs, well beaten
3 squares (1 ounce each)
  unsweetened chocolate
1-1/2 cups ice water
Chocolate Frosting
  (recipe follows)
1/2 cup chopped pecans,
  for garnish

Raisin cream filling
1-1/2 cups milk
3/4 cup granulated sugar
2 tablespoons all-purpose flour
2 egg yolks, beaten

1-1/2 teaspoons vanilla
3/4 cup raisins
3/4 cup chopped pecans

Sift together cake flour, baking soda, baking powder and salt; set aside.

In a large mixing bowl with an electric mixer, cream butter, sugar and vanilla. Add eggs; beat until mixture is light and fluffy.

In a small saucepan (or microwave oven), melt chocolate. Add melted chocolate to batter. Add flour mixture to batter alternately with ice water.

Pour batter into 2 greased and waxed paper-lined 9-inch round cake pans. Bake in a preheated 350-degree oven for 35 to 40 minutes, or until done. Let cool in pans about 5 minutes, then turn out of pans onto racks to cool completely; remove waxed paper. Split cooled layers in half horizontally.

Meanwhile, prepare raisin cream filling. In the top of a double boiler, combine milk, sugar and flour. Slowly add egg yolks. Cook and stir over simmering water until thick. Add vanilla, raisins and pecans. Let filling cool slightly. Spread one-third of filling on each of three cooled cake layers; stack layers. Top with fourth layer (no filling on fourth layer).

Refrigerate cake while preparing Chocolate Frosting. Frost top and sides of cake with frosting. Garnish with chopped pecans. Refrigerate cake until serving time.

Note: Although cake flour is recommended, you can substitute 7/8 cup all-purpose flour plus 2 tablespoons cornstarch for each cup of cake flour.

Chocolate Frosting

1/2 cup margarine	1 teaspoon vanilla
4 tablespoons cocoa powder	1 box (16 ounces)
6 tablespoons milk	confectioners' sugar

In a medium saucepan, combine margarine, cocoa and milk; bring to a boil. Remove from heat; add vanilla and confectioners' sugar, beating constantly.

Use to frost top and sides of Fudge Cake, as directed. (This excellent frosting would be good for any recipe that calls for chocolate frosting.)

Mexican Chocolate Cake

Ann Criswell
Houston Chronicle, Houston, Texas

*The cinnamon and cocoa, historically associated with
Mexico, inspire the name of this rich, luscious cake.*

Makes 15 servings

1/2 cup margarine
1/2 cup vegetable oil
2 squares (1 ounce each)
  unsweetened chocolate (or
  4 tablespoons cocoa powder)
1 cup water
2 cups all-purpose flour
1 teaspoon baking soda
2 cups granulated sugar
1 teaspoon ground cinnamon
1/2 cup sour milk (place 1-1/2
  teaspoons vinegar in a 1/2
  cup measure; fill with milk)
2 eggs, beaten
1 teaspoon vanilla
Mexican Chocolate Icing
  (recipe follows)

Combine margarine, oil, chocolate and water in a saucepan; heat until chocolate is melted.

Combine flour, baking soda, sugar and cinnamon in a large bowl. Stir in sour milk, eggs and vanilla. Blend flour mixture with chocolate mixture.

Pour batter into a greased 15x10x1-inch jelly-roll pan. Bake in a preheated 350-degree oven for 20 to 25 minutes, or until done.

Ice with Mexican Chocolate Icing while cake is still warm and in pan.

Mexican Chocolate Icing

1/2 cup margarine
2 squares (1 ounce each)
  unsweetened chocolate (or 4
  tablespoons cocoa powder)
6 tablespoons milk
1 box (16 ounces)
  confectioners' sugar
1 teaspoon vanilla
1/2 cup chopped pecans

Combine margarine, chocolate and milk in saucepan; heat until bubbles form around the edge. Remove from heat. Add confectioners' sugar, a little at a time. Add vanilla and pecans. Beat well. Use to ice Mexican Chocolate Cake.

Triple Threat Chocolate Cake, Brownies or Truffles

Peggy Rahn
Pasadena Star News, Pasadena, Calif.

For chocoholics, this is a triple treat, depending on how long you bake it. For dieting chocoholics, it becomes a triple threat that you can't resist in any of its delicious forms.

Makes 2 - 10 servings

10 ounces bittersweet chocolate, chopped into 1-inch pieces
1-1/4 cups granulated sugar
1 cup unsalted butter, melted
5 eggs
Pinch salt
1 teaspoon vanilla
Whipped cream or confectioners' sugar, for cake (optional)
Chopped nuts or cocoa powder, for truffles (optional)

Place chocolate and sugar in food processor fitted with the metal blade; process about 1 minute, or until the consistency of sea salt.

Pour melted butter through the feed tube with machine running. Scrape down bowl and process for about 30 seconds. Add eggs, salt and vanilla; process 15 seconds, or until well blended.

Pour batter into a buttered 9-inch springform pan. Place a round of waxed paper directly on top of the batter.

Bake in a preheated 325-degree oven for 45 minutes for a cake, 35 minutes for fudgy brownies, and 30 minutes for truffles. Cool on a rack, remove waxed paper and refrigerate at least 4 hours before serving.

The cake is pretty dusted with confectioners' sugar or topped with a dollop of whipped cream.

For brownies, just cut and serve.

For truffles, form the chilled mixture into balls, using a tablespoon. (Or, you can freeze the baked mixture, then form the frozen mixture into balls. It doesn't get solid, even when frozen.) Roll balls in cocoa powder or finely chopped nuts, if desired.

The number of servings depends on how it's baked and who is eating it.

Raspberry Brownie Torte

Natalie Haughton
Daily News, Los Angeles, Calif.

This torte is a brownie layer topped with a scrumptious chocolate mousse dotted with fresh raspberries. It's a copy of a dessert sampled at a Los Angeles restaurant one summer.

Makes 10 - 12 servings

Brownie base

2 squares (1 ounce each) unsweetened chocolate
1/2 cup butter
2 eggs

1 cup granulated sugar
1-1/2 teaspoons vanilla
1/2 cup all-purpose flour

Mousse topping

1 package (6 ounces) semisweet chocolate morsels
1 square (1 ounce) unsweetened chocolate
1/3 cup hot water
3 egg yolks
1-1/2 teaspoons vanilla
6 tablespoons butter, softened and cut into pieces

1 cup heavy cream
1 pint fresh raspberries, rinsed and drained
1/3 cup granulated sugar (optional)
Whipped cream and chocolate leaves, for garnish (optional)

To make the brownie base, melt chocolate and butter in a small saucepan over low heat or in a glass bowl in the microwave oven. Transfer melted chocolate mixture to a medium mixing bowl. Beat in eggs, sugar and vanilla until well blended. Mix in flour thoroughly. Spread evenly over bottom of a well-buttered 8-inch springform pan. Bake in a preheated 350-degree oven about 25 minutes. Brownie layer should be moist. Do not overbake. Cool in pan.

Meanwhile, prepare mousse topping. Combine semisweet chocolate morsels, unsweetened chocolate and hot water in the bowl of a food processor fitted with a metal blade. Process until mixture is smooth. Add egg yolks and vanilla through feed tube while motor is running. Then add butter, a few pieces at time, until well blended.

Whip cream until stiff. Fold chocolate mixture into whipped cream until well blended. Gently fold in raspberries and sugar, if desired.

Spread mousse mixture evenly over cold brownie layer in springform pan. Cover and refrigerate until firm, several hours or overnight. Serve slices garnished with additional whipped cream and chocolate leaves, if desired.

Note: Torte can be wrapped well and frozen. A couple of hours before serving time, transfer frozen torte to refrigerator to soften.

Black Bottom Cups

Romaine Galey Hon
Idaho Statesman, Boise, Idaho

These cupcakes are favorites with children. I got the recipe from Jacque Burroughs, a former Boise resident who now lives in Denver. She got it from a friend, which proves to me that good cooks like to share recipes.

Makes 24 cupcakes

1 package (8 ounces) cream cheese
1 egg
1-1/3 cups granulated sugar, divided
1/8 teaspoon salt
1 package (6 ounces) semi-sweet chocolate morsels

1-1/2 cups sifted all-purpose flour
1/4 cup cocoa powder
1 teaspoon baking soda
1 cup water
1/3 cup vegetable oil
1 tablespoon vinegar
1 teaspoon vanilla
Additional granulated sugar (optional)

In a medium mixing bowl with an electric mixer, beat cream cheese, egg, 1/3 cup sugar and salt. Stir in chocolate morsels; set aside.

In a large mixing bowl, sift together flour, cocoa, remaining 1 cup sugar and baking soda. Add water, oil, vinegar and vanilla. Beat until well mixed.

Fill 24 greased or paper-lined muffin cups one-third full with chocolate batter. Top each with a heaping spoonful of cream cheese mixture. Sprinkle with additional sugar, if desired. Bake in a preheated 350-degree oven 30 to 35 minutes, or until done.

Bite-Size Cupcakes

Dotty Griffith

Dallas Morning News, Dallas, Texas

This recipe won a reader's recipe contest several years ago. It's the only sweet I make without fail at Christmas.

Makes 70 - 80 bite-size cupcakes

1/2 cup butter
1-1/2 ounces unsweetened baking chocolate
1 cup granulated sugar
2 eggs, beaten

2/3 cup sifted all-purpose flour
1 teaspoon vanilla
1 cup chopped pecans
Dash salt

Frosting
4 tablespoons butter
1/2 ounce unsweetened baking chocolate

2 cups sifted confectioners' sugar
Cold coffee

In a medium saucepan with a heavy bottom, melt butter and chocolate over low heat. Remove from heat; pour over sugar in a medium mixing bowl. Add eggs, flour, vanilla, pecans and salt; blend well.

Place petit four paper baking cups on a cookie sheet. Fill each cup half full with batter. Bake in a preheated 350-degree oven for 10 to 12 minutes, or until done. Let cool, then frost.

For frosting, melt butter and chocolate in a small saucepan. Remove from heat. Add confectioners' sugar and enough cold coffee to make a smooth frosting. Spread frosting on cooled cupcakes.

Chocolate Walnut Torte

Alice Krueger
Winnipeg Free Press, Winnipeg, Manitoba, Canada

This is a European-style torte, very rich with walnuts, chocolate and orange. And, yes, it contains no flour. Because of the amount of walnuts it contains, it is important that the nuts be absolutely fresh. Nothing spoils this cake like rancid or stale walnuts.

Makes 12 - 16 servings

6 eggs, separated
2 cups confectioners' sugar
1/3 cup graham cracker crumbs
2 tablespoons water
1/4 teaspoon cream of tartar

3-1/2 cups finely ground toasted walnuts
1/4 cup orange-flavored chocolate morsels, grated (see note)
Walnut halves, for decoration

Chocolate Glaze
2/3 cup orange-flavored chocolate morsels (see note)

4 tablespoons butter
2 teaspoons honey

In the large mixing bowl of an electric mixer, beat egg yolks until lemon colored. Add sugar; beat on high speed until thick, about 3 minutes. Beat graham cracker crumbs and water into yolk mixture.

In a separate bowl, beat egg whites with cream of tartar until stiff, but not dry. Gently fold beaten egg whites, ground nuts and grated chocolate into yolk mixture. Pour batter into a waxed paper or parchment-lined 9-inch springform pan. Bake in a preheated 350-degree oven for 40 to 50 minutes, or until done. Cool in pan.

Meanwhile, prepare glaze. In the top of a double boiler over hot water or in a microwave oven, melt chocolate morsels and butter. Stir to blend. Stir in honey; mix well.

When cake is cool, invert onto serving plate and remove pan. Pour glaze over cake, covering top and sides. Decorate with walnut halves.

Note: If orange-flavored chocolate morsels aren't available, substitute semisweet chocolate morsels. If desired, add 1/2 to 1 teaspoon grated orange peel, or to taste.

Chocolate Orange Torte

Toni Cashnelli

The Cincinnati Enquirer, Cincinnati, Ohio

Marilyn Harris likes her recipes "elegant, but not in-timidating," and that aptly describes this dessert, which is one of her favorites. Harris makes classic cooking look effortless, as students of her cooking school, L.S. Ayres' Fourth Street Market in Cincinnati, will testify. This cake doesn't look big, but it serves a lot of people because the flavor is intense.

Makes about 16 servings

4 ounces semisweet chocolate
1/2 cup butter, softened
2/3 cup granulated sugar
3 eggs
1 cup ground almonds

1/4 cup very fine dry bread crumbs
Zest of 1 orange
Almonds, for garnish (optional)

Glaze

2 ounces unsweetened chocolate
2 ounces semisweet chocolate

1/4 cup butter
2 teaspoons honey

Melt chocolate in the top of a double boiler over hot, not boiling, water. Cool.

In a large mixing bowl with an electric mixer, cream butter until fluffy. Add sugar, a little at a time, beating constantly. Add eggs, one at a time, beating after each addition. Stir in melted chocolate, ground almonds, bread crumbs and orange zest.

Butter an 8-inch round cake pan and line bottom with buttered waxed paper. Pour batter into pan. Bake in a preheated 375-degree oven for 25 minutes, or until done. Cool 1 hour before turning out of pan.

Meanwhile, prepare glaze by combining chocolates, butter and honey in the top of a double boiler. Cook over hot, not boiling, water until chocolate and butter are melted, stirring occasionally.

Remove top of double boiler from the water. Beat chocolate mixture until cool and glossy.

Pour glaze on completely cooled torte. Garnish with almonds, if desired. Refrigerate just to set glaze. Serve at room temperature.

Schaum Torte
(German Meringue Torte)

Peggy Daum
The Milwaukee Journal, Milwaukee, Wis.

Baked meringue torte has been a classic Milwaukee dessert for decades. In German, "schaum" means "foam." This traditional version came from Ann Hemke, one of the first cooks featured in "Best Cook on the Block," a series that began in the newspaper 10 years ago. Later her recipe was included in the first volume of "The Best Cook on the Block Cookbook."

Her recipe makes individual tortes. Some home cooks prefer to make one large torte and cut it into wedges for serving. While the small tortes are crunchy throughout, the larger torte usually has a soft center. Milwaukeeans have been known to debate which version is better. The answer is: The one your mother made.

Makes 9 individual schaum tortes

3 egg whites
Dash salt
1/2 teaspoon vinegar
1/2 teaspoon vanilla
1 cup granulated sugar

Sweetened strawberries,
or any fruit in season
Whipped cream
9 whole strawberries,
for garnish

In a mixing bowl, beat egg whites with salt until stiff. Add vinegar and vanilla. Add sugar gradually, one teaspoon at a time. Drop meringue by tablespoons onto a greased cookie sheet, or onto a cookie sheet covered with waxed paper.

Bake in a preheated 275-degree oven for 45 minutes. Cool thoroughly.

To serve, make an indentation on top of each meringue shell, using a tablespoon dipped in cold water. Fill indentation with sweetened strawberries. Top each with whipped cream and garnish with a whole strawberry.

Note: The unfilled meringue shells will keep up to 2 weeks if stored in a tightly covered container and kept in a cool, dry place.

Almond Torte with Apricot Butter Cream

Marilyn Myers
Arkansas Gazette, Little Rock, Ark.

If you are looking for a finale to a special dinner, you cannot beat this elegant torte.

Makes 8 - 10 servings

Torte

1-1/2 cups blanched almonds
1 cup granulated sugar, divided

4 tablespoons butter, softened
6 eggs, separated

Apricot butter cream

1/2 cup apricot preserves
1/4 cup water
1 cup butter, softened

4 egg yolks
1 cup confectioners' sugar

For the torte, butter a 15x10x1-inch jelly-roll pan; line the bottom with waxed paper and lightly butter the paper; set pan aside.

Place almonds and 1/2 cup granulated sugar in a food processor or blender. Chop until nuts are ground medium fine. (If using a blender, do in two batches.) Set almond mixture aside.

In a large mixing bowl with an electric mixer, beat butter until light and fluffy. Stir in 3 egg yolks, one at a time, and then half of the almond mixture. Stir in the remaining 3 egg yolks, one at a time, and remaining almond mixture. Mix until smooth; set aside.

In a metal mixing bowl, beat egg whites until stiff. (They will no longer slide in the bowl when bowl is tilted.) Sprinkle 2 tablespoons of the remaining granulated sugar over the egg whites; beat for 10 seconds. Continue this process, until the remaining 6 tablespoons granulated sugar have been added.

Mix a large spoonful of the egg whites into the butter mixture to lighten it; then pour butter mixture into remaining egg whites. Fold just until blended.

Pour batter into prepared pan; tilt it to smooth out the batter. Bake in a preheated 325-degree oven for 20 to 25 minutes, or until lightly browned on top and a finger impression doesn't remain when the cake is lightly touched.

Let cake rest for 15 to 20 minutes, until cool. Turn out of pan and remove waxed paper. Cut cake into 4 lengths that measure 3-3/4 x 10 inches. Keep the pieces touching and side by side.

To make the butter cream, put apricot preserves and water in a small saucepan; cook over low heat until preserves are melted and mixture is blended, stirring occasionally. Pass this mixture through a sieve to remove chunks of pulp; set aside.

In a large mixing bowl with an electric mixer, cream butter until light and fluffy. Beat in egg yolks, one at a time. Gradually stir in confectioners' sugar. Stir in sieved apricot mixture.

To assemble the cake, spread a little more than half of the butter cream over the top of the cake. Stack the 4 layers one on top of the other, making a 4-layer cake. Spread the sides with half of the remaining butter cream. Using a pastry bag fitted with a small star tip, decorate the top and sides of the torte with remaining butter cream.

This cake can be refrigerated or frozen.

Apple Torte

Linda Giuca
The Hartford Courant, Hartford, Conn.

This apple cake has a dense, moist texture and freezes well.

Makes 9 servings

1 cup granulated sugar	1/4 teaspoon salt
1/4 cup butter	1 teaspoon ground cinnamon
1 egg	1/4 teaspoon ground nutmeg
1 teaspoon vanilla	2 cups chopped apples
1 cup all-purpose flour	3/4 cup chopped nuts
1 teaspoon baking soda	Ice cream (optional)

Cream sugar and butter in a mixing bowl; add egg and vanilla. Beat well. Sift together flour, baking soda, salt, cinnamon and nutmeg; stir into egg mixture. Batter will be stiff. Add chopped apples and nuts.

Pour into a greased and floured 8-inch square pan. Bake in a preheated 350-degree oven 45 minutes. Serve warm with ice cream, if desired.

Danish Strawberry Cake

Margaret Kirkwood
Toorak Garden, Australia

This recipe was one that was featured at the Cordon Bleu School of Cooking in London when I studied there in 1960. It has since become a popular recipe with my family and friends here in Australia.

Makes 8 servings

Pastry
1 cup all-purpose flour
6 tablespoons butter, at room temperature
6 tablespoons confectioners' sugar
1 egg yolk
1/2 teaspoon vanilla

Filling
1 cup currant jelly
1 quart fresh strawberries, rinsed and hulled
1 cup heavy cream, whipped

For pastry: Sift the flour onto a pastry board; make a well in the center of the flour. Into this well, place butter, confectioners' sugar, egg yolk and vanilla. Using your hands, work mixture into a smooth dough. (The warmth of your hands helps to blend pastry ingredients.) Set the dough aside in the refrigerator to chill.

Roll the dough into a circle or oblong, 1/4-inch thick. Pinch the edge to decorate; prick the center with a fork. Place dough on a greased baking sheet. Bake in a preheated 375-degree oven for 12 to 15 minutes. Cool on a wire rack.

Place cooled pastry on a serving dish or platter.

For filling: Heat the jelly in a small saucepan. Brush jelly over the pastry shell. Arrange whole strawberries on pastry and brush with remaining jelly. Just before serving, decorate with rosettes of whipped cream or pass whipped cream separately.

Note: This pastry stores well and can be made ahead of time. Other fruits in season can be used, such as large raspberries, pitted sweet cherries, drained canned apricots, pineapple and grapes. Remember to glaze red fruit with red jelly and yellow fruit with an apricot jam or other light-colored jelly, such as lemon-mint or pineapple.

Grandmother's Boiled Raisin Cake

Donna Morgan
The Salt Lake Tribune, Salt Lake City, Utah

This cake always brings back warm, comforting memories of happy times with my grandmother in Rexburg, Idaho. It also brings eating pleasure to my family.

Makes 12 - 15 servings

1 package (16 ounces) raisins
3 cups water
2 cups granulated sugar
1 cup butter or margarine
2 eggs
4 cups all-purpose flour
1 teaspoon baking soda
1/4 teaspoon salt

1/2 teaspoon ground cinnamon
1/2 teaspoon ground nutmeg
1/2 teaspoon ground cloves
1 teaspoon vanilla
1 cup chopped nuts
Confectioner's sugar icing or confectioners' sugar, if desired

In a large saucepan, place raisins, water and sugar; bring to a boil. Reduce heat; simmer 20 minutes. Add butter and stir until melted. Let cool.

Into a large mixing bowl, sift together flour, baking soda, salt, cinnamon, nutmeg and cloves. Add raisin mixture, vanilla, and nuts. Blend well.

Pour batter into a greased and lightly floured 13x9x2-inch baking pan. Bake in a preheated 350-degree oven for 45 minutes, or until cake tests done.

If desired, top with your favorite confectioners' sugar icing or with a sprinkling of sifted confectioners' sugar.

Plum Coffee Cake

Bev Bennett
Chicago Sun-Times, Chicago, Ill.

We don't seem to do enough with Italian plums in the fall, so the Sun-Times developed this plum coffee cake recipe. I tend to think of coffee cake as Midwestern: sweet, unadorned and good.

Makes 12 - 15 servings

2 cups all-purpose flour
1 tablespoon baking powder
1/2 teaspoon salt
3/4 cup granulated sugar
6 tablespoons solid shortening

2 eggs
1 teaspoon vanilla
About 1/2 cup milk
4 to 6 plums

Topping
3/4 cup granulated sugar
1/2 teaspoon ground
cinnamon

1-1/2 tablespoons all-purpose
flour
2 tablespoons butter

Sift flour, baking powder, salt and sugar into a medium bowl. Cut in shortening. Break eggs into a 1-cup measure. Add vanilla to eggs, then fill cup with milk; mix. Stir milk mixture into flour mixture until combined.

Spread batter in a greased 13x9x2-inch baking pan. Cut plums in halves or slices; remove seeds. Arrange plums on top of batter.

To prepare topping, combine sugar, cinnamon, flour and butter in a small bowl; mix with fingers until mixture is crumbly. Sprinkle topping over plums.

Bake in a preheated 350-degree oven for 40 minutes, or until nicely browned.

Cornmeal Pound Cake

Sheryl Julian
Boston Globe, Boston, Mass.

This is an old recipe that I updated for a historical cooking demonstration on cornmeal. The cornmeal gives the pound cake a slightly gritty texture that is pleasing with the buttery crumb.

Makes 6 - 9 servings

1 cup butter, at room temperature
1 cup granulated sugar
4 eggs, lightly beaten
1/2 cup yellow cornmeal

1-1/2 cups all-purpose flour
1-1/2 teaspoons baking powder
1 teaspoon grated nutmeg
3 to 6 tablespoons milk

Generously butter a 9x5x3-inch loaf pan. Line the bottom with waxed paper cut exactly to fit; butter the paper. Dust the inside with flour, tapping out excess flour.

In the bowl of an electric mixer, cream the butter until it is light and fluffy. Add the sugar, a little at a time, beating well after each addition. Pour the eggs into a measuring cup; add them, a spoonful at a time, beating well after each addition.

Combine the cornmeal, flour, baking powder and nutmeg. With the mixer set on its lowest speed, add half the cornmeal mixture to the batter. Then add 3 tablespoons milk, followed by the remaining cornmeal mixture. The batter should just fall from the spoon. Add 1 to 3 additional tablespoons milk, if necessary.

Pour the batter into the prepared pan and smooth the top. Bake in a preheated 350-degree oven for 70 minutes, or until a skewer inserted into the center of the cake comes out clean.

Leave the pound cake in the pan on a rack until it is cool, then turn it out of the pan and let it cool completely. Cut into thick slices and serve.

Sour Cream Pound Cake

Fran Zupan
The Columbia Record, Columbia, S.C.

This recipe comes from Lucille Hanisch who lives in Mayesville, S.C., in a turn-of-the-century home. She enjoys making this cake and others for family and friends. She worked as the cafeteria manager at Mayewood High School for more than 20 years and still cooks Wednesday night dinner at the First Baptist Church in Sumter, S. C.

To keep this cake moist while it is baking, Hanisch suggests placing a shallow pan of water on the lower rack of the oven. She bakes the cake on the upper rack.

Makes 18 - 20 servings

3 cups granulated sugar
1 cup butter, softened
6 eggs, separated
1 teaspoon vanilla
1 teaspoon lemon extract
2 teaspoons butter flavoring

3 cups all-purpose flour
1/2 teaspoon salt
1/4 teaspoon baking soda
1 cup dairy sour cream
Frosting (recipe follows)

In a large mixing bowl with an electric mixer, combine sugar, butter, egg yolks, vanilla, lemon extract and butter flavoring. Beat on low speed for 30 seconds, scraping bowl constantly. Beat on high speed for 2 minutes, scraping bowl occasionally.

Sift together flour, salt and baking soda. Add flour mixture to batter alternately with sour cream.

In a separate bowl, beat egg whites until stiff. Fold egg whites into batter. Pour batter into a greased and floured 10-inch tube pan.

Bake in a preheated 325-degree oven for 1-1/2 to 1-3/4 hours, or until a wooden pick inserted in the center comes out clean. Cool 10 minutes. Remove from pan. Frost cake when cool, if desired, or serve cake plain with fruit.

Frosting

1 box (16 ounces)
 confectioners' sugar
1/2 teaspoon salt
1/3 cup solid shortening

1 teaspoon vanilla
1 teaspoon lemon extract
1 teaspoon butter flavoring
1/4 cup water

In a large mixing bowl with an electric mixer, combine confectioners' sugar, salt, shortening, vanilla, lemon extract, butter flavoring and water. Beat on low speed to blend, then beat on high speed for about 10 minutes, or until frosting is light and very fluffy. Spread on cooled Sour Cream Pound Cake.

Mrs. 'Iggins Icing

Woodene Merriman
The Pittsburgh Post-Gazette, Pittsburgh, Pa.

Back in the days when women went to the beauty shop every Saturday to have their hair "done," the woman under the next dryer most weeks was a Mrs. Higgins. She gave me this recipe. She said it came from a can of Crisco, but how long ago I'll never know. I first printed the recipe in 1966. It is the favorite icing in my family. It's especially good on chocolate cake. Strangely, every time I make it, it is a little different, but every time it's good.

Makes enough to ice a two-layer, 9-inch cake.

2 tablespoons water
4-1/4 tablespoons granulated
 sugar
2-1/3 cups sifted confectioners'
 sugar
1/2 teaspoon salt

1 egg
2/3 cup shortening (half
 margarine or butter and
 half solid shortening)
1 teaspoon vanilla, or more to
 taste

In a small saucepan, boil water and granulated sugar for 1 minute; cool.

In a medium mixing bowl, beat confectioners' sugar and salt with egg. Add sugar syrup; mix well. Then add shortening and vanilla; beat until creamy.

Mocha Pound Cake

Thayer Wine
The Jackson Sun, Jackson, Tenn.

This recipe was a prize winner several years ago in a mayonnaise recipe contest. I have made it often not only to serve to company, but also to take to school bake sales where it always gets raves.

Makes 12 - 16 servings

5 eggs
3 cups granulated sugar
1-1/2 cups mayonnaise
  (not salad dressing)
2 teaspoons vanilla
2 cups unsifted all-purpose
  flour
1 cup unsweetened cocoa
  powder
1/2 teaspoon baking powder
1/2 teaspoon baking soda
1/4 teaspoon salt
2 tablespoons instant coffee
  powder
1/4 cup very hot water
1 cup buttermilk or sour milk
Confectioners' sugar or
  whipped cream (optional)

Grease and flour a 10-inch tube pan or two 9x5x3-inch loaf pans; set aside.

In a large bowl with electric mixer on high speed, beat eggs, sugar, mayonnaise and vanilla for about 4 minutes, or until light and fluffy.

Sift together flour, cocoa, baking powder, baking soda and salt.

Dissolve coffee in hot water; stir into buttermilk until well mixed.

Reduce speed of mixer to low; add flour mixture alternately with coffee mixture to egg mixture, beating just until well blended. Pour batter into prepared pan(s).

Bake on center rack of a preheated 325-degree oven 1 hour and 15 minutes (50 to 60 minutes for loaf pans), or until cake tester inserted in center comes out clean.

Cool in pan(s) 10 minutes. Remove from pan(s). Cool completely on wire rack. If desired, sprinkle with confectioners' sugar or serve with a dollop of whipped cream.

Note: This cake freezes well.

Blueberry Cheesecake

Barbara McQuade

The Vancouver Sun, Vancouver, British Columbia, Canada

British Columbia grows more blueberries than any other province in Canada. This cheesecake with blueberry sauce is popular for entertaining.

Makes 12 servings

Crust

1-1/2 cups graham cracker crumbs

1/2 teaspoon ground cinnamon

1/2 cup margarine or butter, melted

Filling

2 packages (8 ounces each) cream cheese

2 tablespoons all-purpose flour

1 cup granulated sugar

5 medium eggs, well beaten

2 cups dairy sour cream

Glaze

3 cups fresh blueberries, divided

1/2 cup water

1/3 cup granulated sugar

2 tablespoons cornstarch

For the crust, combine cracker crumbs with cinnamon and melted margarine in a mixing bowl; mix well. Spread in bottom and up sides of a 9-inch springform pan. Bake in a preheated 350-degree oven for 10 minutes. Cool.

For the filling, beat cream cheese in a large mixing bowl with an electric mixer until fluffy. Beat in flour and sugar. Beat in eggs until mixture is smooth. Stir in sour cream until well blended.

Pour filling into crust. Bake in a preheated 350-degree oven for 50 to 55 minutes, or until set in the center. Cool, then chill well. Just before serving, remove pan sides.

For the glaze, place 2 cups blueberries and water in a saucepan; bring to a boil, then simmer gently 1 minute. Mix sugar and cornstarch; stir into simmering blueberries. Cook, stirring, until mixture is thickened and clear. Stir remaining 1 cup blueberries into glaze. Let stand until cold.

Spread on enough blueberry glaze to cover top of cheesecake. Any remaining glaze can be served separately.

Heath Bar Mocha Cheesecake

Natalie Haughton
Daily News, Los Angeles, Calif.

This sensational cheesecake is designed for Heath bar and mocha lovers. It's a copy of a cheesecake available at a Los Angeles dessert place that specializes in cheesecakes. If you make the dessert ahead of time and freeze it, be sure to add the Heath bars to the top just before serving. Otherwise, you'll lose the crunchy texture of the candy bars.

Makes 12 - 16 servings

1 package (8-1/2 ounces) chocolate wafers
3 tablespoon butter, melted
8 (1-3/16 ounces each) original Heath English Toffee candy bars, divided
1-1/3 cups heavy cream, divided
5 tablespoons instant dry coffee crystals (use decaffeinated, if desired)

3 packages (8 ounces each) cream cheese, at room temperature
1 cup granulated sugar
4 eggs
1 tablespoon vanilla
1 package (11.5 ounces) milk chocolate morsels (2 cups)

In a food processor fitted with a steel blade, process wafers until fine crumbs are formed. Mix with melted butter; press into bottom and part way up the sides of a greased 9-1/2-inch springform pan. Finely chop 4 of the Heath bars; sprinkle chopped candy over crust. Refrigerate while preparing filling.

Heat 1/2 cup cream in top of double boiler or in microwave oven just until hot enough to dissolve instant coffee. Stir in coffee. Refrigerate until cool, about 15 minutes.

Meanwhile, in a bowl of an electric mixer, beat cream cheese and sugar until smooth. Beat in 1/2 cup cream, eggs and vanilla until well mixed. Slowly beat in coffee-cream mixture and continue beating 10 minutes. Turn mixture into candy-topped crust.

Bake in a preheated 325-degree oven 1 hour and 15 to 20 minutes, or until cake looks set around the edges and center jiggles slightly. Cool cake before refrigerating.

Combine milk chocolate morsels and remaining 1/3 cup cream in the top of a double boiler or in microwave oven; heat until smooth when stirred. Cool in refrigerator until thick enough to spread over cheesecake.

Spread cooled chocolate mixture over cooled cheesecake. Break remaining 4 Heath bars into bite-size pieces; sprinkle over cheesecake. Refrigerate until chocolate layer is set and cake is well chilled.

Italian Cheesecake

Evelyn Cairns
Mellus News-Herald/Newspapers, Wyandotte, Mich.

I've never tasted a cheesecake I didn't like, but my all-time favorite was shared by a reader, Angelina Dalton of Lincoln Park, Mich., in 1969. It can be served with a fruit topping, but I personally would not think of masking its luscious lemon flavor.

Makes 12 - 15 servings

1 pound ricotta cheese
1 pound cream cheese
1-1/2 cups granulated sugar
4 eggs, slightly beaten
1 teaspoon vanilla
1 teaspoon lemon extract
  (not lemon juice)

3 tablespoons all-purpose flour
3 tablespoons cornstarch
1/2 cup butter, melted and
  cooled
2 cups dairy sour cream
Graham cracker crumbs

In a large mixing bowl with an electric mixer, cream ricotta cheese and cream cheese. Add sugar, eggs, vanilla and lemon extract; mix well. Add flour and cornstarch, then add melted butter. Fold in sour cream.

Grease a 9-inch springform pan and sprinkle generously with graham cracker crumbs. Pour cheese mixture into pan.

Bake in a preheated 325-degree oven for 1 hour. Then turn off the heat and leave cake in oven for 2 hours. Do not open the oven door for 3 hours after the cake is placed in the oven. This is the most important step of the recipe.

After 3 hours, remove cheesecake from oven and cool completely. Store in refrigerator until ready to serve.

Pumpkin Cheesecake

Judy Hille Walker
The Arizona Republic, Phoenix, Ariz.

This cheesecake was developed by pastry chef Jimmy Johnson at the Phoenix Hyatt Regency. He wowed a luncheon group by serving the sauce in hollowed-out mini pumpkins. I'll never make another pumpkin pie for Thanksgiving.

Makes 8 servings

Crust
1 cup graham cracker crumbs
1 tablespoon granulated sugar
2 tablespoons melted butter or margarine

Filling
3 packages (8 ounces each) cream cheese, at room temperature
1 cup granulated sugar
1 cup dairy sour cream
1 teaspoon vanilla
1 tablespoon pumpkin pie spice
6 eggs
1 cup canned pumpkin

Cranberry Sauce
(recipe follows)

For the crust, combine crumbs, sugar and melted butter. Mix well. Spread evenly in a 9-inch pie pan; set aside.

For the filling, combine cream cheese and sugar in the large mixing bowl of an electric mixer. Beat with electric mixer on medium speed until mixture is light and creamy. Add sour cream; mix 1 minute. Add vanilla and pumkin pie spice; mix 1 minute. Add eggs; mix 1 minute. Add pumpkin; mix 2 minutes.

Pour filling into graham cracker crust. Bake in a preheated 375-degree oven for 45 minutes, or until firm.

Chill in refrigerator overnight. Serve with Cranberry Sauce.

Cranberry Sauce

1 quart water
1 package (12 ounces) fresh cranberries
1 cup granulated sugar
1 teaspoon lemon juice
1 teaspoon almond extract, or to taste

In a large saucepan, combine water, cranberries, sugar and lemon juice. Bring to a boil; boil until berries are soft to the touch. Drain the juice into a bowl; reserve juice.

Puree cranberries in a blender or food processor. Combine puree and reserved juice. Flavor with almond extract to taste. Chill.

When ready to serve Pumpkin Cheesecake, pour some Cranberry Sauce over each serving.

Fresh Ginger Cake

Barbara McQuade
The Vancouver Sun, Vancouver, British Columbia, Canada

Ginger — fresh, preserved or crystallized — is a popular spice in British Columbia. This cake using fresh ginger is light and not too sweet. It's good with whipped cream.

Makes 9 servings

1-1/2 cups all-purpose flour
1 teaspoon baking soda
1/4 teaspoon salt
7 tablespoons vegetable oil
1/2 cup plus 1 tablespoon
   apple juice
1/2 cup packed brown sugar
1/4 cup molasses

1/4 cup dark corn syrup
1 egg
3 tablespoons grated fresh
   ginger root
Whipped cream (optional)
Finely chopped crystallized
   ginger (optional)

Combine flour, baking soda and salt; set aside.

In a large mixing bowl, combine oil and apple juice. Beat in brown sugar, molasses and corn syrup. Beat in egg. Add grated ginger and reserved flour mixture; mix well.

Grease a 9-inch square baking pan; line bottom with waxed paper. Pour batter into pan. Bake in a preheated 350-degree oven for 30 to 35 minutes, or until cake is firm to the touch in the center and has pulled away slightly from the sides of the pan.

Cool in the pan on a wire rack about 5 minutes, then turn out onto rack. Cut into squares and serve warm or at room temperature. Garnish with whipped cream and a sprinkle of finely chopped crystallized ginger, if desired.

Dark Orange Cake

Wanda A. Adams
Seattle Post-Intelligencer, Seattle, Wash.

This recipe is stamped indelibly on my brain: When I first published it, in March, 1985, I left out the flour!

I was out of the office the morning the recipe ran and the receptionist was at the point of answering the phone with "two cups of flour" by the time I returned.

After the correction was printed, I received numerous calls and letters praising the cake. It has a lovely balance of sweetness with bitterness and piquancy with richness. And, yes, you do use the whole orange.

The recipe is the invention of Terry Hopkins, of Oreas Island, Wash. It won a local dairy recipe contest.

Makes 15 servings

1 cup granulated sugar
1/2 cup butter, softened
2 eggs
1 teaspoon vanilla
2 cups all-purpose flour
1 teaspoon baking soda
1 teaspoon baking powder

1/2 teaspoon salt
1 cup buttermilk, at room temperature
1 cup raisins
1 cup walnuts
1 whole, large orange, cut into chunks

Orange Frosting

2 cups sifted confectioners' sugar
2 tablespoons butter, softened
1 teaspoon vanilla

2 to 3 tablespoons dairy sour cream
2 tablespoons reserved orange mixture (from preparing cake)

Butter and flour a 13x9x2-inch glass cake pan. Set aside.

In the large bowl of an electric mixer, cream sugar, butter and eggs; add vanilla.

Stir or sift together flour, baking soda, baking powder and salt. Add flour mixture alternately with the buttermilk to the creamed mixture, stirring well after each addition.

In a food processor or grinder, finely grind the raisins, nuts and orange (peel and all). Reserve 2 tablespoons of this mixture for the orange frosting. Add the remaining ground orange mixture to the batter.

Spread batter in prepared pan. Bake in a preheated 350-degree oven for 40 to 50 minutes, or until a toothpick inserted near the center comes out clean. Cool in pan on rack.

Meanwhile, prepare orange frosting. In a medium bowl, beat confectioners' sugar, butter and vanilla. Add enough sour cream to achieve a spreading consistency. Stir in reserved ground orange mixture.

Spread frosting on cooled cake.

Clove Cake

Marlene Parrish
Pittsburgh Magazine, Pittsburgh, Pa.

This is a wonderful dessert for holiday dinners. It's festive and smells old fashioned.

Makes 12 - 15 servings

1 teaspoon vinegar
About 1 cup milk
1 cup butter
2-1/4 cups granulated sugar
5 eggs
3 cups all-purpose flour

1 tablespoon ground cloves
1 tablespoon ground cinnamon
1/8 teaspoon salt
1 teaspoon baking soda
Sweetened whipped cream
(optional)

Make sour milk by placing vinegar in a glass measuring cup. Fill with milk to measure 1 cup. Stir, then let stand 5 minutes.

In a large mixing bowl with an electric mixer, cream butter with sugar until smooth. Add eggs, one at a time, beating well after each addition.

Combine flour, cloves, cinnamon and salt. Add about one-third of the flour mixture to the butter mixture. Stir in 1/2 cup sour milk. Add another one-third of the flour mixture; mix well.

Stir baking soda into remaining 1/2 cup sour milk; mix into the batter along with remaining flour mixture.

Pour batter into a greased 10-inch tube or Bundt pan. Bake in a preheated 350-degree oven for 45 to 50 minutes, or until cake tests done. Cool cake 10 minutes in the pan. Then remove from pan and cool on a wire rack. Serve with whipped cream, if desired.

Oatmeal Cake

Barbara Hertenstein
St. Louis Post-Dispatch, St. Louis, Mo.

This is my mother's popular oatmeal cake with a double-thick coconut and pecan topping. The cake is simple to make, but it's easy to burn the topping. Take the phone off the hook and don't answer the door while it's under the broiler. As tempting as it might be to walk away, the only way to be sure the topping doesn't end up a burned, black crust is to stand at the oven door and watch it.

Makes 35 squares

1 cup quick-cooking rolled oats
1/2 cup butter
1-1/4 cups boiling water
1 cup granulated sugar
1 cup firmly packed brown sugar
2 eggs

1 teaspoon vanilla
1-1/3 cups all-purpose flour
1/2 teaspoon salt
1 teaspoon baking soda
1/2 teaspoon ground nutmeg
1 teaspoon ground cinnamon

Topping
1/2 cup plus 2 tablespoons butter, melted
1/3 cup light cream or milk
1 teaspoon vanilla
1/2 cup granulated sugar

1/3 cup brown sugar
1 to 1-1/2 cups chopped pecans
1-3/4 to 2 cups flaked coconut

To prepare the cake, combine oats, butter and boiling water in a medium mixing bowl. Let stand 20 minutes.

In a large mixing bowl with an electric mixer, combine granulated sugar, brown sugar and eggs. Add vanilla. Blend in flour, salt, baking soda, nutmeg and cinnamon. Add to oat mixture. Beat with electric mixer on medium speed for 3 minutes.

Spread batter in a greased and floured 15x10x1-inch jelly roll pan. Bake in a preheated 350-degree oven 30 to 35 minutes, or until cake tests done.

While cake is baking, prepare topping. In a medium bowl combine butter, cream, vanilla, granulated sugar, brown sugar, pecans and coconut.

Spread topping on hot cake. Slide cake under hot broiler, 4 to 5 inches from heat. Broil 8 to 10 minutes, or until lightly browned. Watch closely; the topping browns quickly. Turn pan during broiling, if necessary. Cool cake in pan; cut into squares to serve.

Banana Split Cake

Janice Okun
Buffalo News, Buffalo, N.Y.
This easy cake is well loved in Buffalo.

Makes 20 - 24 squares

Crust

3/4 cup butter or margarine, melted

3 cups graham cracker crumbs

Filling

1 cup margarine or butter
2 cups confectioners' sugar
2 eggs
1 teaspoon vanilla
6 or 7 bananas
Lemon juice
1 can (20 ounces) crushed pineapple, well drained

2 cups sweetened whipped cream, prepared whipped topping mix or frozen whipped topping, thawed
Chopped nuts, for garnish
Sliced maraschino cherries, for garnish

For the crust: Combine melted butter and crumbs. Press against bottom and up the sides of a 13x9x2-inch pan.

For the filling: Combine margarine, sugar, eggs and vanilla in a mixer bowl. Beat 20 minutes with an electric mixer, or until mixture is light and very fluffy. Spread in crust.

Meanwhile, peel bananas; slice crosswise. Dip in lemon juice. Arrange banana slices on sugar mixture. Spread well-drained pineapple over bananas. Spread whipped cream over pineapple. Sprinkle with nuts and sliced cherries.

Chill several hours or overnight. Cut into small squares to serve.

Texas Carrot Cake

Karen Haram

San Antonio Express-News, San Antonio, Texas

Because carrots are a big crop from August to May in different areas of Texas, cooks are always looking for tasty ways to use them. One of my favorites is this cake recipe that includes the unusual addition of German sweet chocolate. This recipe originally came from Arlene Lightsey, who writes a weekly column for the paper in which she searches out and tests reader-requested chefs' recipes.

Makes 12 - 15 servings

Fine dry bread crumbs, for dusting cake pan
3 cups sifted all-purpose flour
2 cups granulated sugar
1 square (1 ounce) German sweet chocolate, grated
2 teaspoons ground cinnamon
1-1/2 teaspoons baking soda
1-1/2 teaspoons salt
1 teaspoon baking powder

1 can (8 ounces) crushed pineapple
3 eggs, beaten
1-1/2 cups vegetable oil
2 teaspoons vanilla
2 cups grated raw carrots
1-1/2 cups finely chopped pecans
Icing (recipe follows)

Butter a 10- to 12-cup tube or Bundt pan. Dust with fine dry bread crumbs. Invert pan and tap out excess crumbs. Set aside.

In a large mixing bowl, combine flour, sugar, grated chocolate, cinnamon, baking soda, salt and baking powder. Drain pineapple, saving syrup. Add syrup to flour mixture. Add eggs, oil and vanilla. Beat on medium speed of an electric mixer for 3 minutes. Stir in pineapple, carrots and pecans.

Pour batter into prepared pan. Bake in a preheated 350-degree oven for 75 to 90 minutes, or until cake tests done. Cool in pan 10 minutes before removing from pan. Ice with icing.

Icing

2-1/4 cups confectioners' sugar
4 ounces (1/2 of an 8-ounce package) cream cheese, softened
3 tablespoons butter, softened
1 tablespoon vanilla
1 tablespoon milk
1/4 cup chopped pecans
1/4 cup currants (optional)

In a medium mixing bowl, combine sugar, cream cheese, butter, vanilla and milk; mix until smooth. Add pecans and currants, if desired.

Use to ice Texas Carrot Cake.

Poppy Seed Cake

Marty Meitus
Rocky Mountain News, Denver, Colo.

This recipe came from a friend who picked it up while living in New Mexico. My friend added more poppy seeds for extra taste. It's a very stiff, heavy batter that produces a wonderful cake for snacks, brunch or even special dinners.

Makes 16 servings

4 cups all-purpose flour
2 cups granulated sugar
1 teaspoon salt
4 teaspoons baking powder
2 eggs, well beaten
1 can (12 ounces) evaporated milk
2 cups vegetable oil
2 teaspoons vanilla
1 cup poppy seeds

In a large mixing bowl, combine flour, sugar, salt and baking powder. In another bowl, beat eggs, then gradually add evaporated milk, oil and vanilla. Fold flour mixture into egg mixture. Add poppy seeds. Pour batter into a greased 10-inch tube or Bundt pan.

Bake in a preheated 350-degree oven for 50 minutes, then reduce oven temperature to 325 degrees and continue baking for 25 to 30 minutes. Do not open oven to check until cake has baked for 65 minutes.

Devil's Food Cake

Rosemary Black
The Record, Hackensack, N.J.

My great-aunt Hazel was one of the best bakers I have known, and this cake was one of her all-time success stories. All of my sisters — and I have seven of them — have copied down the recipe at one time or another. It is unbelievably easy. I have substituted plain yogurt or coffee-flavored yogurt for the buttermilk with good results.

Makes 12 - 16 servings

1-1/2 cups granulated sugar
1 cup solid shortening or butter, softened
3 eggs, well beaten
1 teaspoon baking soda
1 cup buttermilk or sour milk
2-1/2 cups sifted all-purpose flour
3 heaping tablespoons cocoa powder
1 teaspoon salt
1 teaspoon baking powder
3/4 cup hot water
1 teaspoon vanilla
Chocolate Cream Cheese Frosting (recipe follows)

In the large mixing bowl of an electric mixer, cream sugar and shortening. Add the eggs; beat well. Add the baking soda to the buttermilk; add to sugar mixture and mix well. Combine sifted flour, cocoa, salt and baking powder; sift into batter. Beat well. Add hot water and vanilla. Beat well.

Pour batter into 2 greased and floured 8- or 9-inch round cake pans. Bake in a preheated 350-degree oven for about 30 minutes, or until cake tests done. Cool in the pans for 10 minutes. Remove from pans and cool completely on wire racks. Fill and frost with Chocolate Cream Cheese Frosting.

Chocolate Cream Cheese Frosting

Makes enough frosting for a 2-layer (8- or 9-inch) cake

1 package (3 ounces) cream cheese, softened
About 1 tablespoon milk
1-1/2 teaspoons vanilla

2 cups confectioners' sugar
2 squares (1 ounce each) unsweetened baking chocolate, melted and cooled

In a small bowl with an electric mixer, beat cream cheese, milk and vanilla until smooth. Add confectioners' sugar and continue beating until frosting is smooth. Add melted chocolate; mix well. If necessary, add a little more milk until frosting is of spreading consistency.

Use to fill and frost Devil's Food Cake.

Hawaiian Wedding Cake

Evelyn Cairns
News-Herald Newspapers, Wyandotte, Mich.

This cake is a favorite in our area, and it is so simple to make.

Makes 12 - 15 servings

1 cup margarine
2 cups granulated sugar
5 eggs
2 teaspoons baking powder
1 pound graham cracker crumbs
1 cup milk

1 can (3-1/2 ounces) flaked coconut
1 cup chopped nuts
1 can (20 ounces) crushed pineapple, well drained
Whipped cream (optional)

In a large mixing bowl with an electric mixer, cream margarine and sugar until well blended. Add eggs; mix well. Combine baking powder and crumbs; add to sugar mixture. Slowly add milk, coconut, nuts and pineapple. Batter will look curdled.

Pour batter into a greased and floured 13x9x2-inch baking pan. Bake in a preheated 375-degree oven for 40 to 50 minutes, or until done. Cool slightly in pan before cutting into squares. Serve with whipped cream, if desired.

Never-Fail Passover Sponge Cake

Janet Beighle French
Plain Dealer, Cleveland, Ohio

Every Passover, the Plain Dealer food staff used to get queries about sponge cakes that fell out of the pans as soon as the cakes were turned over.

Then a local musician, Mildred Zimbalist, came to everyone's rescue by sharing a recipe for a cake that will NEVER fall out. So far, this cake has lived up to its reputation. Now, the Passover brings requests for this cake.

Makes one 10-inch cake

8 eggs, separated
1 cup plus 1 tablespoon granulated sugar, divided
1/2 cup matzo cake meal (finer than matzo meal)
1/4 cup potato starch
1/8 teaspoon salt
1/4 cup lemon juice
Grated peel of 1/2 lemon

Set out the egg whites for 2 hours to warm up.

Beat egg whites until foamy, then gradually beat in 1/2 cup sugar; beat until stiff peaks form that are white and shiny, but not dry. Refrigerate, if you want a super-duper cake.

Sift together cake meal, potato starch and salt; set aside.

Beat egg yolks with remaining 9 tablespoons sugar, until well blended. Add lemon juice. Beat until thick and lemon colored. Stir in lemon peel.

Add sifted cake meal mixture, 1 tablespoon at a time, to egg yolk mixture, folding in after each addition.

Remove egg whites from refrigerator. Fold in yolk mixture.

Turn batter into 10-inch tube pan that has never been greased and is very clean. Bake in a preheated 325-degree oven for about 50 minutes, or until cake tests done with a toothpick.

Immediately invert on pan legs, or slide tube of pan over bottle with pan inverted. Let cool thoroughly. Then run knife around between cake and pan. Remove cake. Serve cake upside down.

Cookies

Butterscotch Date Bars
Cherry Drop Cookies
Clara's Crispy Cookies
Cowboy Cookies
Cucidati
Date Cookies
Double Chocolate Brownies
Double Treat Cookies
German Chocolate Cake Cookies
Ginger Snaps
Graham Cracker Brownies
Lebkuchen
Lemon Squares
Linzer Hearts
Mandel Bread
Mom's Jelly Cookies
Nanaimo Bars
Oleycoecks
Pecan Dreams
Sand Tarts
Snowball Meltaways
Spiced Apple Drops
Super Chocolate Chip Cookies
Texas Tassie Bars

Double Treat Cookies

Rosemary Black
The Record, Hackensack, N.J.

This recipe is from my aunt Puthie. It makes a wonderful lunchbox treat. It's a great cookie to make with children because the dough is sturdy enough to withstand handling by children. The cookies freeze well, too.

Makes about 7 dozen

2 cups sifted all-purpose flour
2 teaspoons baking soda
1/2 teaspoon salt
1 cup solid shortening
1 cup granulated sugar
1 cup firmly packed brown sugar
2 eggs
1 teaspoon vanilla
1 cup peanut butter
1 cup chopped, salted peanuts
1 package (6 ounces) semi-sweet chocolate morsels
Additional granulated sugar

Sift together flour, baking soda and salt; set aside. In a mixing bowl with an electric mixer, cream shortening with granulated sugar and brown sugar. Add eggs; beat until fluffy. Blend in vanilla, then the peanut butter. Add flour mixture; beat well. Stir in the peanuts and chocolate morsels.

Shape dough into small balls; place balls on ungreased baking sheets. Flatten balls with a glass that has been dipped in granulated sugar.

Bake in a preheated 350-degree oven for about 8 minutes, or until golden brown.

Lemon Squares

Mary Lou Montgomery
Hannibal Courier-Post, Hannibal, Mo.

This is a very rich and tasty dessert that is simple to prepare. Most cooks have all the ingredients in their kitchens.

Makes about 24 squares

1 cup butter
2 cups plus 4 tablespoons all-purpose flour, divided
1/2 cup confectioners' sugar
4 eggs
4 tablespoons lemon juice
2 cups granulated sugar
1 teaspoon baking powder
1/2 teaspoon salt
Additional confectioners' sugar

Melt butter in a 13x9x2-inch baking pan. Add 2 cups flour and 1/2 cup confectioners' sugar; mix. Pat down flat in pan. Bake in a preheated 350-degree oven for 20 minutes.

Meanwhile, in a medium mixing bowl, beat eggs and lemon juice until light. Sift together remaining 4 tablespoons flour, granulated sugar, baking powder and salt. Add to egg mixture. Mix well. Pour over hot crust. Return to 350-degree oven and bake 25 minutes. Sprinkle confectioners' sugar over top. Cut into squares while hot.

Super Chocolate Chip Cookies

Karen Haram
San Antonio Express and News, San Antonio, Texas

This recipe is one both kids and adults love. Cooks enjoy it, too, because it goes together in less than 10 minutes. I like to bake this huge cookie in disposable aluminum pizza pans, decorate it or personalize it with chocolate icing, and take it to birthday parties or children's school activities.

Like many of my family's favorites, this recipe was shared by a San Antonian, Vernie Jo Wagner, who was featured in our "Best Cook on the Block" monthly column.

Makes 16 - 20 wedges

1/4 cup granulated sugar
1/3 cup brown sugar
1/2 cup margarine, softened
1 egg
1 teaspoon vanilla
1-1/3 cups all-purpose flour

1/2 teaspoon baking soda
1/4 teaspoon salt
1/2 cup chopped pecans or walnuts
3/4 cup semisweet chocolate morsels

In a large bowl with an electric mixer on high speed, cream sugars and margarine until light. Beat in egg and vanilla. On low speed, add flour, baking soda and salt. Mix well. Fold in nuts and chocolate morsels.

Spread the dough on a greased 12- or 13-inch round pizza pan. Bake in a preheated 350-degree oven for 15 to 18 minutes, or until lightly browned. Do not overbake. Cool, then slice into wedges or bars.

German Chocolate Cake Cookies

Barbara Gibbs Ostmann
St. Louis Post-Dispatch, St. Louis, Mo.

These cookies were "invented" by a friend, Susan Manlin Katzman, the day of a Christmas cookie exchange. She combined several recipes to produce these mouth-watering gems, which won first prize at the party.

Makes 6½ dozen

Dough

4 cups all-purpose flour
1/4 cup unsweetened cocoa powder
1 teaspoon salt
2 cups confectioners' sugar
2 cups butter, softened
4 teaspoons vanilla

Filling

2/3 cup undiluted evaporated milk
2/3 cup granulated sugar
2 egg yolks, beaten
1/3 cup butter
1 teaspoon vanilla
3/4 cup chopped pecans
1-1/4 cups shredded coconut

Topping

1/2 cup semisweet chocolate morsels
2 tablespoons water
2 tablespoons butter
1/2 cup sifted confectioners' sugar

For the dough, sift together flour, cocoa and salt. In a large mixing bowl with an electric mixer, cream confectioners' sugar, butter and vanilla until light. Blend flour mixture into butter mixture. Dough will be stiff. Use your hands to knead the ingredients together, if necessary. If not well mixed, parts of the dough will be too soft and other parts too dry and crumbly.

Using about 2 tablespoons dough, form dough into balls. Put balls on ungreased baking sheets; make an indentation in center of each ball with your finger. Bake in a preheated 350-degree oven about 12 to 14 minutes, or until cookies are slightly browned around edges. Remove from baking sheets immediately and cool on wire racks.

For the filling, combine milk, sugar, egg yolks, butter and vanilla in a saucepan. Cook, stirring constantly, over medium heat. In about 5 to 8 minutes, mixture will be slightly thick and gold in color. Mixture will get thicker as it cools. Remove from heat; add pecans and coconut. Let cool about 15 to 20 minutes, then drop a small amount of filling in the indentation in each cookie. Let cool.

For the topping, combine chocolate morsels, water and butter in a saucepan. Heat, stirring constantly, until smooth. Add sugar and beat until smooth. Drizzle topping over cookies.

Store in airtight tins or freeze.

Graham Cracker Brownies
Sharon Hudgins
The Stars and Stripes, West Germany

The taste of these brownies never fails to bring back the memory of cool autumn days in Texas, when my mother would bake these as a treat for us after school. They are especially easy to make from ingredients Mother always seemed to have on hand.

Makes 16 very rich brownies

1 can (14 ounces) sweetened condensed milk (not evaporated milk)
2 teaspoons vanilla
1/2 teaspoon salt

1 package (6 ounces) semi-sweet chocolate morsels
1 cup coarsely chopped pecans
2 cups graham cracker crumbs (made from approximately 24 2-inch graham crackers)

Butter very heavily the bottom and sides of an 8-inch square baking pan.

In a large bowl, mix together the sweetened condensed milk, vanilla and salt. Stir in chocolate morsels, pecans and graham cracker crumbs. Mix with a wooden spoon until all the ingredients are well blended. The dough will be very stiff.

Put the dough in the prepared pan, and use your hands to pat it into an even layer. Bake in a preheated 350-degree oven (325 degrees if using a glass baking pan) for 20 to 25 minutes. Let the brownies cool to room temperature in the pan, then cut them into 2-inch squares.

Double Chocolate Brownies

Maxine Levy
Dallas, Texas

My daughter, Jayn, is credited with bringing home this recipe, which I have used many times with great success. Jayn first sampled the brownies when she and Tori Foster were freshmen at Wellesley College. Tori's mother, Kay Foster, of Duxbury, Mass., made them for the girls. She later shared the recipe. The brownies are incredibly fudgy and easy to make.

Makes 36

4 squares (1 ounce each) unsweetened chocolate
1/2 cup unsalted butter
4 eggs, at room temperature
2 cups granulated sugar
1 cup sifted all-purpose flour
1 teaspoon vanilla
6 ounces (1 cup) semisweet chocolate morsels

In the top of a double boiler over 1 to 2 inches of simmering (not boiling) water, melt unsweetened chocolate and butter. (If desired, melt chocolate and butter in a microwave oven by putting ingredients in a small glass bowl and cooking, uncovered, on Medium, or 50 percent, power for 4 minutes, or until smooth.) Remove from heat and let cool slightly.

In a large mixing bowl with an electric mixer on medium speed, beat eggs until frothy. Gradually add sugar. Stir in melted chocolate mixture; blend well. Gradually add flour, mixing well after each addition. Stir in vanilla and chocolate morsels.

Butter the bottom and sides of a 9-inch square pan. Spread batter evenly in pan. Bake in a preheated 325-degree oven for 35 to 37 minutes. Do not overbake. Mark into squares while hot. A metal right-angle "brownie lifter" makes removing the first square easy.

Texas Tassie Bars

CiCi Williamson
MicroScope, Alexandria, Va.

The pecan is the state tree of Texas. Where I grew up in Dallas, Pecan Tassies (bite-size pecan pies) were popular at tea time. I have adapted the recipe so it can be made in one panful and cut into bars, instead of preparing individual little pies. Also this recipe can be made in a microwave oven.

Makes about 36 bars

1 cup plus 3 tablespoons all-purpose flour, divided
2/3 cup light brown sugar, divided
1/4 teaspoon baking powder
1/2 cup margarine, softened

1-1/4 cups pecan pieces, divided
2 eggs, lightly beaten
3/4 cup dark corn syrup
1 teaspoon vanilla
1/4 teaspoon salt

Put 1 cup flour, 1/3 cup brown sugar and baking powder in a bowl or food processor. Stir or pulse briefly. Add margarine; mix with hands until crumbly or pulse in the food processor. Add 1/4 cup pecan pieces; mix or pulse. Press into the bottom of an 8- inch square glass baking dish. Bake in a preheated 350-degree oven for 15 minutes; cool 5 minutes.

Meanwhile, combine remaining 1/3 cup brown sugar and remaining 3 tablespoons flour in a small mixing bowl. Add eggs, corn syrup, vanilla and salt; mix well.

Gently pour mixture over baked crust; sprinkle with remaining 1 cup pecan pieces. Bake in a preheated 350-degree oven 20 to 25 minutes, or until pecan mixture is set. Cool 2 hours before cutting into bars.

Microwave directions: Prepare crust as directed. Microwave on High (100 percent) power for 6 to 8 minutes, rotating dish several times during baking. Prepare pecan filling as directed. Microwave on Medium-High (70 percent) power for 7 to 9 minutes, rotating dish twice during cooking. Cool 2 hours before cutting into bars.

Clara's Crispy Cookies

Jann Malone
Richmond Times-Dispatch, Richmond, Va.

These cookies are a cook's security blanket — comforting protection against the next midnight cookie attack. With a roll of dough in the freezer, you can have cookies ready in about 15 minutes. The slice-and-bake approach is also perfect for small families who can't eat eight dozen cookies in one sitting.

This recipe comes, via a Richmond friend, from a good cook in Binford, N.D. The original version is not an icebox cookie recipe, but it makes a good one. The logs of unbaked cookie dough will keep in the freezer for about six months.

Makes 8 dozen

1 cup margarine, softened
1 cup vegetable oil
1 cup granulated sugar
1 cup lightly packed dark brown sugar
1 egg
1 teaspoon vanilla
1 cup crispy rice cereal

1 cup flaked coconut
1 cup quick-cooking rolled oats
1/2 cup finely chopped pecans
3-1/2 cups sifted all-purpose flour
1 teaspoon salt
1 teaspoon cream of tartar
1 teaspoon baking soda

In a large bowl with an electric mixer, cream margarine; gradually beat in oil, granulated sugar, brown sugar, egg and vanilla. Beat until mixture is light and fluffy. Stir in cereal, then coconut, then oats, then pecans.

In a separate bowl, mix flour, salt, cream of tartar and baking soda. Gradually add the flour mixture to the margarine mixture; stir until everything is well mixed and no traces of flour remain. Chill dough in bowl for 1 hour.

Divide dough into 4 parts. With lightly floured hands, shape each mound of dough into a log about 6 to 7 inches long and about 1-1/2 to 2 inches in diameter. Wrap each log in plastic wrap and freeze. For long-term freezing, double-wrap in aluminum foil or plastic bags. This dough must be frozen — refrigerated dough is still too soft to slice.

With a serrated knife, thinly slice frozen logs about 1/8- to 1/4-inch thick. Place slices an inch apart on ungreased cookie sheets. Bake in a preheated 350-degree oven for 8 to 10 minutes, or until cookies are lightly browned at edges. Eat straight from the oven or cool on paper towels or wire racks.

Pecan Dreams

Lorrie Guttman
Tallahassee Democrat, Tallahassee, Fla.

Pecans grow well in North Florida, and there are many recipes that make use of them. This bar cookie recipe was submitted as part of our bi-monthly Capital Chef recipe contest. These cookies taste like pecan pie.

Makes about 24 cookies

First layer
1/2 cup butter
1/4 cup confectioners' sugar

1 cup minus 2 tablespoons all-purpose flour

Second layer
2 eggs
2 tablespoons all-purpose flour
1/2 teaspoon baking powder

1-1/2 cups firmly packed brown sugar
1 cup coarsely chopped pecans

For the first layer, combine butter, sugar and flour in a medium mixing bowl. Mix until thoroughly blended. Pat mixture into the bottom of an ungreased 13x9x2-inch baking pan.

For the second layer, beat eggs lightly in a small bowl. Sift together flour and baking powder. Add flour mixture and brown sugar to eggs. Mix until smooth. Stir in pecans. Spread this mixture over the first layer in the pan.

Bake in a preheated 375-degree oven for 30 to 40 minutes, or until golden brown and set. Cool. Cut into squares.

Cowboy Cookies

Romaine Galey Hon
Idaho Statesman, Boise, Idaho

Children love these cookies — I think the name adds to the appeal. The recipe, which appeared in one of my food articles, comes from the Morrison-Knudsen's cafeteria in Boise.

Makes 5 dozen

1-1/2 cups margarine
1-1/2 cups granulated sugar
1-1/2 cups firmly packed
  brown sugar
3 eggs
1-1/2 teaspoons vanilla
3 cups all-purpose flour
3/4 teaspoon baking powder

1-1/2 teaspoons baking soda
3/4 teaspoon salt
1 cup chopped nuts
3 cups quick-cooking
  rolled oats
1 cup semisweet chocolate
  morsels

In a large mixing bowl with an electric mixer, beat together margarine, granulated sugar, brown sugar, eggs and vanilla. Add flour, baking powder, baking soda, salt and nuts; mix well. Add oats and chocolate morsels. Chill dough in refrigerator for several hours.

Roll dough into 1-inch balls. Flatten with palm of hand and put on ungreased cookie sheets. Bake in a preheated 350-degree oven for 8 to 10 minutes, or until done.

Snowball Meltaways

Bev Bennett
Chicago Sun-Times, Chicago, Ill.

This recipe comes from a reader of our "swap shop" column. Variations of this recipe have made the rounds in Chicago for years, but this version happens to be the best I've ever tasted.

Makes about 3 dozen

1 cup unsalted butter
1/4 cup sifted confectioners'
  sugar, plus extra for
  rolling cookies

1 teaspoon vanilla
1-3/4 to 2 cups sifted
  unbleached flour
1/2 cup chopped pecans

In a heavy saucepan over low heat, melt butter until light brown. Pour into a small bowl, discarding any sediment on the bottom. Chill until firm.

Cream butter, 1/4 cup sugar and vanilla until light and fluffy. Add flour. Blend in pecans. Chill until firm.

Shape dough into 1-inch balls. Place balls on an ungreased cookie sheet. Bake in a preheated 350-degree oven for 15 minutes. Remove from the cookie sheet and cool on wire racks. When cool, roll in confectioners' sugar.

Sand Tarts

Louis Mahoney
The Richmond News Leader, Richmond, Va.

These cookies are made everywhere and they are called everything from Sand Tarts to Mexican Wedding Cookies, but when I think of Christmas cookies, these are among the first that come to mind. I can't remember a year without them.

Makes 3 - 4 dozen

1 cup butter	1 teaspoon vanilla
1/2 cup confectioners' sugar	Dash salt
2 cups sifted cake flour	Confectioners' sugar
1 cup chopped pecans	

In a large mixing bowl with an electric mixer, cream butter and 1/2 cup confectioners' sugar. Mix in flour, pecans, vanilla and salt. Roll into balls or shape into crescents. Place on ungreased cookie sheets.

Bake in a preheated 325-degree oven for 20 minutes, or until very lightly browned. While cookies are still warm, roll in additional confectioners' sugar.

Spiced Apple Drops

Ginger Johnston
The Oregonian, Portland, Oregon

Apples and apple juice along with hazelnuts, which also are known as filberts, abound in the Northwest in the fall. So this recipe, which came from a staff member, is a favorite fall cookie in our area.

Makes about 4½ dozen

1/2 cup butter or margarine, softened
1-1/2 cups firmly packed brown sugar
2 eggs
1/2 teaspoon salt
1 teaspoon ground cinnamon
1/2 teaspoon ground nutmeg
1/4 teaspoon ground cloves

2-3/4 cups sifted all-purpose flour
1 teaspoon baking soda
1/2 cup apple juice
1 teaspoon vanilla
1/2 cup raisins
1/2 cup currants
1 cup chopped hazelnuts (filberts)

Apple glaze
1/3 cup margarine
2 cups confectioners' sugar

1 teaspoon vanilla
2 tablespoons apple juice

In a large mixing bowl with an electric mixer, cream butter, brown sugar, eggs, salt, cinnamon, nutmeg and cloves until blended and fluffy. Add flour, baking soda, apple juice, vanilla, raisins, currants and hazelnuts; mix well. (If dough is soft, cover and refrigerate.)

Drop dough by rounded teaspoonfuls about 2 inches apart on greased cookie sheets. Bake in a preheated 375-degree oven for 10 to 12 minutes, or until done. Let cool on wire racks.

While cookies are baking, prepare apple glaze. Heat margarine over low heat until golden brown; remove from heat. Stir in confectioners' sugar and vanilla. Beat in apple juice until mixture is smooth and of desired consistency.

Glaze cooled cookies with apple glaze.

Ginger Snaps

Julian Armstrong
The Gazette, Montreal, Quebec, Canada

Make these crisp cookies in a small size and enjoy them with coffee or tea, or make large ones and fill them with lightly sweetened whipped cream — a luxurious dessert. A tip from my mother, who taught me this family recipe while I was growing up in Toronto: To retain the crisp quality of the cookies, store them in closely covered containers. They will keep for about a week this way. If you're serving them filled with whipped cream, fill them just before serving. Do not freeze.

Makes about 50 small or 36 large cookies

1/2 cup molasses
1/2 cup butter
1 cup all-purpose flour
2/3 cup granulated sugar

1-1/2 teaspoons ground ginger
1 teaspoon lemon juice
1/4 teaspoon vanilla

In a medium saucepan, heat molasses until it bubbles. Add butter, stirring until it melts. Remove from heat. Sift together flour, sugar and ginger; blend into molasses mixture. Stir in lemon juice and vanilla. At this point, batter can be refrigerated for a day.

When ready to bake cookies, grease 2 cookie sheets. Arrange 6 half-teaspoonfuls of batter 4 inches apart on cookie sheet, if making small cookies. Arrange 6 heaping teaspoonfuls of batter 5 inches apart, if making large cookies.

Bake in a preheated 300-degree oven 5 to 8 minutes, or until batter has spread and is bubbling and browned. Have several wooden spoons ready. Let cookies cool on cookie sheets for almost 1 minute, or until you can lift edge of cookie with spatula without pushing it out of shape. Working quickly, roll each cookie around handle of a wooden spoon. Leave on spoon and set aside on wire rack until crisp and dry, about 5 minutes. Continue baking in small batches. After a few rounds, you will become an expert. If cookie hardens too much to roll, return it to the oven for a few seconds and try again.

Linzer Hearts

Sheryl Julian

The Boston Globe, Boston, Mass.

These heart-shaped cookies are made to resemble the classic jam-filled Linzer Torte. Many bakeries make and sell these sandwiched sugar cookies, which can be reproduced easily at home. They are especially good for Valentine's Day.

You will need two heart-shaped cutters, one about 2-1/2 to 3 inches at the widest point, the other 1-1/2 to 2 inches at the widest point.

Makes 14 sandwich cookies and 14 tiny plain hearts

1/3 cup unsalted butter, at room temperature
1/3 cup granulated sugar
2 egg yolks
1-1/2 cups all-purpose flour
Pinch salt
1 tablespoon ice water

Granulated sugar, for rolling cookies
1/3 cup seedless red raspberry jam
Confectioners' sugar, for sprinkling

With an electric mixer, cream the butter until it is soft and light. Add the sugar; continue beating until it is all incorporated. Add the egg yolks, one at a time, then beat in the flour, salt and ice water. When the mixture is not quite smooth, remove the beaters from the bowl and turn the dough out onto a counter sprinkled lightly with flour.

Knead the dough lightly half a dozen times, until you can form it into a smooth, flat cake. Wrap it tightly in plastic wrap and refrigerate it for 20 minutes.

Sprinkle a pastry board or a clean countertop lightly with granulated sugar. Roll out the dough to 1/8-inch thickness.

Use the larger cutter to stamp out 28 hearts, reshaping and rerolling the scraps when necessary. Use a wide metal spatula to transfer 14 of the hearts to a very lightly buttered baking sheet.

Use the smaller cutter to stamp out the centers of the remaining 14 hearts. Carefully transfer both the small centers and the heart borders to the baking sheet.

Bake in a preheated 375-degree oven for 8 to 10 minutes, or until cookies are barely golden on the edges.

Remove from the baking sheet and transfer to wire racks to cool completely.

Use the small hearts as is. Assemble the remaining hearts in the following way: Set the large whole hearts on a board and use a small metal palette knife to spread them with raspberry jam to within 1/4 inch of the edge. Put a heart frame on top of each jam-covered heart; press them together very gently. Sprinkle the edges of the sandwiched cookies with confectioners' sugar and serve at once. The cookies can be stored in an airtight container for several days.

Mom's Jelly Cookies

Elaine Corn
Sacramento Bee, Sacramento, Calif.

My mother, Vivienne Corn, always made these cookies for special occasions such as weddings or bar mitzvahs. They look very pretty on a dessert table and taste even better.

Makes 2 dozen

2 cups all-purpose flour
2/3 cup granulated sugar
1/2 teaspoon baking powder
3/4 cup butter, softened

1 egg
2 teaspoons vanilla
Dark jelly or preserves, such as raspberry or blackberry

In a medium mixing bowl, combine flour, sugar and baking powder. Blend in butter with a pastry cutter. Add egg and vanilla; mix to form a dough. If dough is soft, chill.

Divide dough into 4 parts. Shape each part into a 13-inch rope 3/4-inch thick. Place rolls 2 at a time on ungreased cookie sheets. Using the blunt end of a kitchen knife, make a lengthwise indentation down the center of each roll. Fill indentation with jelly. Bake in a preheated 350-degree oven for 15 to 20 minutes. Cookies will spread. Cool no more than 5 minutes before cutting. Cut diagonally. Cool completely.

Cherry Drop Cookies

Nancy Weir
Gwinnett Daily News, Lawrenceville, Ga.

Cherry Drop Cookies mean Christmas to me. My mother, Evelyn Glover, earned a measure of fame in our neighborhood for the variety of Christmas cookies that she would offer to friends who dropped by during the holidays. Often there were 20 kinds from which to choose — crisp meringue cookies, chewy date pinwheels, traditional European cookies, three-layer chocolate bars and more.

Today I cannot afford the time or the calories to make all those cookies, so I have chosen my favorite from that colorful platter of goodies, and I make these cookies every year.

Makes 40 cookies

1 cup margarine
1-1/2 cups granulated sugar
2 eggs
2 tablespoons milk
1 teaspoon vanilla

1 teaspoon almond extract
2-1/2 cups all-purpose flour
1/2 teaspoon baking powder
1 teaspoon salt
Candied red and green cherries, halved

In a large mixing bowl with an electric mixer, cream margarine and sugar. Add eggs; beat until fluffy. Add milk, vanilla and almond extract; mix well. Add flour, baking powder and salt; blend thoroughly.

Drop by teaspoonfuls onto greased cookie sheets. Top each with a cherry half. Bake in a preheated 375-degree oven for 10 to 12 minutes, or until lightly browned.

Date Cookies

Rosemary Black
The Record, Hackensack, N.J.

This is a soft, moist cookie — very old fashioned and wholesome. It comes from my aunt's friend, Angelita, who was really like an aunt to me.

Makes about 4 dozen

2 cups dates
3/4 cup granulated sugar
3/4 cup water
1 cup softened shortening (butter, margarine or solid shortening)
2 cups firmly packed light brown sugar
1/2 cup buttermilk, sour milk or water
1 teaspoon vanilla
3-1/2 cups all-purpose flour
1 teaspoon salt
1 teaspoon baking soda
1/4 teaspoon ground cinnamon

In a medium saucepan, combine the dates, granulated sugar and water. Cook until thick, stirring constantly. Set aside to cool.

In a mixing bowl, combine the softened shortening, brown sugar and buttermilk. Beat well. Add the vanilla. Sift together the flour, salt, baking soda and cinnamon. Add flour mixture to creamed mixture; beat well.

Drop teaspoonfuls of dough 2 inches apart on greased cookie sheets. Drop approximately 1/2 teaspoon of date filling on top of each cookie. Cover date filling with 1/2 teaspoon dough.

Bake in a preheated 375-degree oven for 10 minutes. Be careful not to let them burn. Cool on wire racks.

Butterscotch Date Bars

Barbara Gibbs Ostmann
St. Louis Post-Dispatch, St. Louis, Mo.

Each year on the first Wednesday of December, we publish the annual Christmas cookie section. Readers contribute their family-favorite recipes and we test and taste them before sharing them with all the readers via the cookie section. Each year, we come across some new and wonderful cookies, as well as the usual classic favorites.

This cookie is sort of a sleeper. It doesn't sound that great — but it is, especially after it ages for about two days (if eaten right after baking, it is rather plain). Because it is a bar cookie, it is quick and easy — something most holiday bakers appreciate.

Makes about 36

1/3 cup margarine, softened
3/4 cup granulated sugar
2 eggs
1/3 cup butterscotch topping
1/2 teaspoon vanilla
3/4 cup all-purpose flour
1/2 teaspoon baking soda
1/2 teaspoon salt
1 cup chopped dates
1/2 cup chopped pecans or other nuts
Confectioners' sugar

Combine margarine and sugar. Beat in eggs, butterscotch topping and vanilla. Add flour, baking soda and salt; mix well. Fold in chopped dates and nuts.

Pour mixture into greased 9-inch square pan. Bake in a 350-degree oven for 30 minutes. Let cool. Cut into squares. Toss squares in confectioners' sugar.

These cookies are best if they age in an airtight container (a plastic bag works well) for about two days before eating. They are moist, soft and chewy.

Oleycoecks

Peter G. Rose

Gannett Westchester Rockland Newspapers, New York

This recipe, from America's Dutch colonial past, is adapted from a recipe found in Anna De Peyster's (1701-1774) handwritten cookbook, which is in the Sleepy Hollow Restoration's collection. Oleycoecks were a favorite treat then, and can still be now. They are an excellent item for a bake sale or other fund-raiser. They can be made several days ahead. Store in a covered container or freeze.

Makes about 30

2 packages active dry yeast
1/4 cup warm water (105 to 115 degrees)
Pinch granulated sugar
1/2 cup butter
3/4 cup granulated sugar

3 eggs
1 cup milk
4 cups all-purpose flour
Vegetable oil for deep-frying
Additional granulated sugar to coat finished product

In a small bowl, sprinkle yeast on water and add a pinch of sugar; set aside.

In a large mixing bowl, beat butter, 3/4 cup sugar and eggs. Add milk and yeast mixture; mix well. Slowly add flour and combine thoroughly. Let the dough rise until double in bulk.

Heat oil to 350 to 360 degrees in a deep-fryer or saucepan.

Form dough into about 30 balls. Using 2 tablespoons, drop balls into hot fat; cook a few at a time, but do not crowd them in the fat. Cook slowly on one side until a deep brown, then turn and cook on the other side. Remove from fat and drain on a thick layer of paper towels. Roll in granulated sugar to coat. Cool and serve.

Cucidati

Sharon Sanders
Chicago Sun-Times, Chicago, Ill.

*This recipe for Cucidati, Sicilian fig cookies, was in
the Sun-Times' top 10 recipes of 1986.*

Makes about 4 dozen

Pastry dough (recipe follows)
1/4 pound walnut halves or
   hazelnuts, toasted
   (see note)
1/2 pound dried figs, trimmed
   of stems, halved
1/2 cup seedless raisins
Grated rind of 1 orange
1/4 cup water

1/2 cup honey
1/2 teaspoon ground
   cinnamon
1-1/2 cups confectioners' sugar
3 tablespoons plus 1 teaspoon
   freshly squeezed lemon juice
Multi-colored candy sprinkles
   (optional)

Prepare pastry dough and refrigerate at least 30 minutes.

Meanwhile, in a food processor fitted with a steel blade or with a food grinder, grind nuts until finely chopped. Add figs, raisins and orange rind to bowl or grinder. Process or grind until mixture is coarse and sticks together like a paste. Place fig mixture in a mixing bowl.

In another small bowl, whisk water into honey gradually until well incorporated. Stir cinnamon into honey mixture. Gradually stir honey mixture into fig mixture.

Divide chilled pastry into thirds. Refrigerate remaining dough while working with one piece. Dough will be soft and a bit sticky.

Roll dough on a well-floured work surface to 1/16-inch thickness. Cut dough with a 2-1/4-inch round cutter. Place 2 level teaspoons fig filling in the center of each of half the dough rounds. Cover with remaining dough rounds. Press dough edges down around filling and then press with a fork to seal the dough rounds together. Dip fork in flour frequently to prevent sticking. Place cookies on lightly greased baking sheets.

Bake in a preheated 400-degree oven for 10 minutes, or until bottoms are golden and tops are set. Remove from oven to cool.

Continue with remaining dough and filling until all cookies are made. Dough scraps can be chilled for 15 minutes and then rerolled.

Combine confectioners' sugar with lemon juice to make a glaze. Drizzle glaze over cookies. Decorate immediately with candy sprinkles, if desired. When glaze sets, store cookies in a tin.

Note: To toast nuts, spread them in a single layer on a baking sheet. Place in a preheated 400-degree oven for about 10 minutes, or until nuts are golden. Remove from baking sheet to cool. If using hazelnuts, rub nuts in a dish towel to remove skins.

Pastry For Cucidati

2-1/2 cups sifted all-purpose flour
1/2 cup granulated sugar
2-1/2 teaspoons baking powder
1/4 teaspoon salt

1/2 cup cold butter or margarine
2 eggs
1/4 cup milk
1/2 teaspoon vanilla

Sift flour, sugar, baking powder and salt into a medium mixing bowl. Cut in butter with pastry blender until mixture resembles coarse cornmeal.

In a small bowl or cup, lightly beat eggs with milk and vanilla. Stir milk mixture into flour mixture. Turn dough onto a work surface and knead lightly with your hands until dough forms a ball. Chill for 30 minutes.

Use as directed to make Cucidati.

Nanaimo Bars

Barbara McQuade
The Vancouver Sun, Vancouver, British Columbia, Canada

These dessert bars — a cross between a cookie and a candy — are a tradition in British Columbia at Christmas time. Nanaimo is the name of a city on Vancouver Island. The recipe dates back to the '50s in our files, but the origin is unknown. Many different versions exist — mocha, mint, etc., but the original is still the favorite.

Makes about 36 bars

3/4 cup plus 1 tablespoon butter, divided
1/4 cup granulated sugar
1 egg
5 tablespoons cocoa powder
2 cups graham cracker crumbs
1/2 cup flaked coconut
1/2 cup chopped nuts

3 tablespoons milk
2 tablespoons vanilla custard powder (see note)
2 cups sifted confectioners' sugar
4 squares (1 ounce each) semi-sweet chocolate

In the top of a double boiler, combine 1/2 cup butter, granulated sugar, egg and cocoa. Place over boiling water and stir until the mixture resembles a custard. Remove from heat; add crumbs, coconut and nuts. Spread in a buttered 13x9x2-inch baking pan. Press down. Refrigerate.

In a medium mixing bowl, combine 1/4 cup butter, milk, custard powder and confectioners' sugar. Beat to make a smooth mixture. Spread over the crumb base in the pan. Refrigerate to harden this layer.

In the top of a double boiler over hot water, melt chocolate and remaining 1 tablespoon butter. Spread over the confectioners' sugar mixture. Refrigerate.

Note: Custard powder is a Canadian product that is sometimes available at gourmet shops in the United States. If you cannot find custard powder, substitute 2 tablespoons instant vanilla pudding and pie filling mix (dry).

Lebkuchen

Jane Baker
The Phoenix Gazette, Phoenix, Ariz.

It wouldn't be Christmas without these moist German cookies. My grandmother always made them for Christmas and I have carried on the tradition. They have to be made well in advance of the holiday and stored in airtight containers with an apple slice to soften them.

Makes 5 - 6 dozen

2/3 cup honey
1 cup granulated sugar
1/3 cup butter
1 egg
1/3 cup water
4 cups all-purpose flour
1 teaspoon baking soda

1 teaspoon ground cinnamon
1 teaspoon ground cloves
2/3 cup chopped nuts
1/3 cup chopped candied citron
Confectioners' sugar glaze
Red or green colored sugar

In a medium saucepan, combine honey, sugar and butter. Bring to a boil; boil for 5 minutes, stirring occasionally. Cool.

In a mixing bowl, combine egg and water; beat well with an electric mixer. Sift together flour, baking soda, cinnamon and cloves. Add flour mixture to egg mixture alternately with honey mixture. Beat well after each addition. Stir in nuts and citron.

Cover dough with plastic wrap and allow it to ripen 3 or 4 days in the refrigerator.

To bake the cookies, shape dough into small balls, put balls on ungreased cookie sheet, and flatten balls with the bottom of a glass. Bake in a preheated 350-degree oven for 10 to 15 minutes, or until done.

Store cookies with apple slices in covered containers for several weeks to soften. After baking, the cookies are hard and crisp. They are ready to eat when they are soft and moist. You might have to change the apple slices after several weeks.

Before serving, frost with confectioners' sugar glaze made by combining confectioners' sugar with enough milk to make a rather thin glaze. If desired, sprinkle moist glaze with red or green colored sugar.

Mandel Bread

Janet Beighle French
Plain Dealer, Cleveland, Ohio

The best homemade Mandel Bread we've ever tasted showed up unexpectedly at a press party at the Cleveland Institute of Music.

It had been made by Estelle Berman, secretary to Institute president Grant Johannesen and the widow of a viola player with the New York Philharmonic.

Mrs. Berman bakes her cookies in old, metal ice-cube trays. We baked them in trays (from a flea market) and in loaf pans. The latter work fine, although the cookies aren't shaped quite as nicely. This is her recipe.

Makes about 5 dozen slices

3 eggs
1 cup plus 2 teaspoons granulated sugar, divided
1 cup vegetable oil
1 teaspoon vanilla
2 teaspoons lemon juice

3 cups all-purpose flour
1/2 teaspoon baking powder
1/4 teaspoon salt
1 cup finely chopped nuts
1/2 teaspoon ground cinnamon

Grease three metal ice-cube trays or three 8-1/2x4-1/2x2-1/2-inch loaf pans.

With an electric mixer, beat together eggs and 1 cup sugar. Slowly beat in oil, then vanilla and lemon juice.

Sift or sieve flour, baking powder and salt into a bowl. Add flour mixture slowly to egg mixture, beating in on very low speed. Stir in nuts. Divide batter among prepared trays or loaf pans.

Bake in a preheated 375-degree oven for about 17 minutes, or until batter pulls away from pans and feels done on top. Let cool in pans about 15 minutes. Reduce oven temperature to 250 degrees.

Turn flat cookie "loaves" out of pans. Slice 1/2-inch thick. Place slices one layer deep on ungreased baking sheets. Mix remaining 2 teaspoons sugar and cinnamon; sprinkle over slices. Dry cookie slices in 250-degree oven for about 10 minutes.

Puddings & Soufflés

Almendrado with Custard Sauce
Apple Sundae Pudding
Banana Pudding
Bread Pudding with Orange Butter Sauce
Creme Brulée
Double Chocolate Pudding
Lemon Sponge Pudding
Orange Sponge
Princess Rice

Apple Sundae Pudding

Sue Dawson
The Columbus Dispatch, Columbus, Ohio

Falling leaves and cool nights bring to mind apple orchards, the spicy scent of cinnamon and desserts warm from the oven. This old-fashioned dessert fills the bill perfectly.

Makes 6 servings

2 cooking apples
1 cup all-purpose flour
2 teaspoons baking powder
3/4 teaspoon salt, divided
1 teaspoon ground cinnamon
2/3 cup plus 1/4 cup granulated sugar, divided
1/2 cup milk
1/2 cup chopped walnuts

2 tablespoons melted butter or margarine
1-1/2 teaspoons vanilla, divided
1/2 cup firmly packed brown sugar
1 cup boiling water
Whipped cream (optional)

Core, peel and slice apples. Place in the bottom of a 2-quart baking dish.

Sift flour, baking powder, 1/2 teaspoon salt, cinnamon and 2/3 cup granulated sugar into a large mixing bowl. In a separate bowl, combine milk, walnuts, butter and 1 teaspoon vanilla. Stir milk mixture into flour mixture; spread on top of apples in baking dish.

Mix together brown sugar, remaining 1/4 cup granulated sugar, remaining 1/2 teaspoon vanilla and remaining 1/4 teaspoon salt. Sprinkle over batter in baking dish. Pour boiling water over all. Do not stir.

Bake, uncovered, in a preheated 350-degree oven for 30 minutes. Cover and bake 30 minutes longer. Serve warm with whipped cream, if desired.

Banana Pudding

Louis Mahoney
The Richmond News Leader, Richmond, Va.

This is a true Southern classic, which practically every household has made at one time or another. The recipe originally came from a box of vanilla wafers.

Makes 8 servings

4 eggs
3/4 cup granulated sugar, divided
3 tablespoons all-purpose flour
Dash salt

2 cups milk
1/2 teaspoon vanilla
Vanilla wafers
5 to 6 medium-size, fully ripe bananas, peeled and sliced

Separate 3 of the eggs. In the top of a double boiler, combine 1/2 cup sugar, flour and salt. Mix in 1 whole egg and 3 egg yolks. Stir in milk. Cook over boiling water, stirring constantly, until thickened. Remove from heat and stir in vanilla.

Spread a small amount of custard on the bottom of a 1-1/2-quart casserole dish. Cover with a layer of wafers and top with a layer of sliced bananas. Pour about one-third of the custard over the bananas. Continue layering wafers, bananas and custard to make 3 layers of each, ending with custard.

Beat 3 egg whites until stiff, but not dry. Gradually add remaining 1/4 cup sugar and beat until mixture forms stiff peaks.

Pile meringue on top of pudding being careful to cover the entire surface. Bake in a preheated 425-degree oven about 5 minutes, or until delicately browned. Serve warm or chilled.

Almendrado

Judy Hille Walker
The Arizona Republic, Phoenix, Ariz.

*Since practically everybody in our state has moved
here from somewhere else, it's unusual to find natives.
My former roommate, Christia Johnson Gibbons, is such
a rare bird. She was born and raised in Tucson, and for
Mexican dinner parties she makes this almond pudding
that is typical of the area. It's a light conclusion to a meal,
and the colors represent the Mexican flag. This version,
unlike many recipes, relies on almonds instead of
almond flavoring, which gives the dessert added texture
and interest.*

Makes 6 - 8 servings

2 envelopes unflavored gelatin
1/4 cup cold water
1/4 cup boiling water
6 egg whites (save yolks for
   custard sauce recipe which
   follows)

1-1/2 cups granulated sugar
1 teaspoon vanilla
4 ounces almonds, ground or
   chopped
Red and green food coloring
Custard Sauce (recipe follows)

In a small bowl, soften gelatin in cold water; then add boiling
water and stir until gelatin is dissolved. Cool.

In a large mixing bowl with an electric mixer, beat egg whites until
stiff. Gradually add sugar and vanilla, then slowly beat in cooled
gelatin; beat until mixture stands in peaks.

Divide mixture evenly among 3 separate bowls. To one part, add
the almonds. Tint one part pink with red food coloring; tint the
remaining part mint green with the green food coloring.

Line a glass 9x5x3-inch loaf pan with waxed paper, letting some
paper drape over the edges for easy removal. Spread the pink mixture in the bottom of the pan, then add the white almond mixture.
Top with the green mixture, making three layers. Cover and
refrigerate until ready to serve.

To serve, pull pudding out of pan with waxed paper. Cut into
1-inch slices. Top each serving with Custard Sauce.

Custard Sauce

6 egg yolks
1/4 cup granulated sugar
1/2 teaspoon salt
2 cups milk

1/2 teaspoon almond extract
2 tablespoons butter or
  margarine

In the top of a double boiler, combine egg yolks, sugar and salt; mix well. Stir in milk. Cook, stirring constantly, over hot, not boiling, water until mixture thickens enough to coat the back of a metal spoon in a velvety layer. Add almond extract and butter; stir until butter melts.

Set top of double boiler in a pan of cold water and stir to cool. Cover and chill. Serve over Almendrado.

Lemon Sponge Pudding

Marcia Bennett
Pittsburgh Post-Gazette, Pittsburgh, Pa.

This recipe was my mother's, printed on a yellowing, dog-eared card which I inherited along with all of her other great recipes. This is a light, refreshing dessert which is easy to make and can be served warm or cold. It is one of the few homemade desserts I make which serves a small family.

Makes 4 servings

1 tablespoon all-purpose flour
1/2 cup granulated sugar
2 tablespoons lemon juice

Grated peel of 1 lemon
  (about 1-1/2 teaspoons)
2 eggs, separated
1 cup milk

In a 3-cup ovenproof casserole dish, combine flour, sugar, lemon juice and lemon peel; mix well.

Beat egg yolks until lemon colored; add to milk. Add egg mixture to flour mixture, stirring until well blended. Beat egg whites until stiff; fold into custard mixture.

Place casserole in a pan of hot water. Bake in a preheated 350-degree oven for 35 to 40 minutes, or until nicely browned. Serve warm or cold in sherbet glasses.

Bread Pudding

Helen Austin
Arkansas Democrat, Little Rock, Ark.

Zinzendorf's was a restaurant in Conway, a college town about 30 miles from Little Rock. The couple who owned the restaurant, Don and Nancy Bingham, also gave cooking classes, including classes for children (they have five of their own). They sold the restaurant so Don could go to seminary, but their recipe for bread pudding is still one of my favorites.

Makes 10 - 12 servings

1 loaf (about 12 ounces) French bread, torn or cut into 1 or 2 inch pieces
1/3 cup raisins
1/2 cup butter or margarine, melted
2 cups heavy cream
2 cups milk
4 eggs

1 teaspoon vanilla
1 cup granulated sugar
3/4 cup brown sugar
1 teaspoon ground cinnamon
1 teaspoon ground nutmeg
Orange-Butter Sauce (recipe follows)
Whipped cream, for garnish (optional)

Place bread pieces in a large, generously buttered 13x9x2-inch baking dish. Sprinkle raisins over bread pieces. Drizzle melted butter over bread, mixing with hands to coat evenly.

In a medium mixing bowl, beat cream, milk, eggs and vanilla. Add granulated sugar, brown sugar, cinnamon and nutmeg; blend well. Pour over bread mixture in pan. Let bread soak, pressing it gently to insure complete soaking, until there is little or no liquid in bottom of pan.

Put pan with bread mixture in a larger pan; fill pan with water halfway up the sides of bread-filled pan. Bake in a preheated 350-degree oven for 45 to 60 minutes, or until well browned and risen as a souffle.

Serve warm or at room temperature, accompanied by Orange Butter Sauce and, if desired, whipped cream.

Orange-Butter Sauce

1/4 cup butter or margarine
3/4 cup granulated sugar

1/2 cup dairy sour cream
2 tablespoons orange juice

In a medium saucepan, melt butter. Add sugar, sour cream and orange juice. Bring to a boil; cook, stirring constantly, until mixture is slightly thickened.
Serve with Bread Pudding.

Orange Sponge

Mary Ann Dedow
Oshkosh Northwestern, Oshkosh, Wis.

This is an easy dessert that I got from my mother, Henrietta Hanseter. It makes a nice light dessert in the summertime.

Makes 6 servings

3/4 envelope unflavored gelatin
1/2 cup cold water
1-1/2 cups mandarin oranges, drained
1 cup mandarin orange juice
1/2 cup finely chopped pecans

2 bananas, peeled and sliced thin
1/4 cup granulated sugar
1 tablespoon lemon juice
1 cup heavy cream, whipped
Mayonnaise
Additional mandarin orange slices for garnish, if desired

Soak gelatin in water 5 minutes. Drain oranges, saving 1 cup juice. Put juice in a medium saucepan. Heat juice slightly, then add gelatin mixture and stir to dissolve. Remove from heat. Add mandarin oranges, pecans, bananas, sugar and lemon juice. Mix well. Chill until partly set, stirring occasionally. Fold in whipped cream. Pour into a 1-1/2-quart mold that has been lightly greased with mayonnaise.

Chill overnight. Unmold on a decorative plate. Garnish with additional orange slices, if desired.

Double Chocolate Pudding

Richard Sax
New York City, N.Y.

Nowadays, you can get chocolate mousse nearly everywhere. But when was the last time you had real homemade chocolate pudding?

Makes 4 servings

2-1/4 cups milk, divided
1/2 cup granulated sugar, divided
Pinch salt
2 tablespoons cornstarch, sifted
3 tablespoons best-quality cocoa powder
1 egg

2 egg yolks
5 ounces best-quality semi-sweet chocolate, chopped
2 tablespoons unsalted butter, cut up
1 teaspoon vanilla
Whipped cream, for garnish

In a heavy saucepan, bring 2 cups milk, 1/4 cup sugar and salt to a boil over medium heat.

In a large mixing bowl, whisk together cornstarch, cocoa and the remaining 1/4 cup sugar until well combined and free of lumps. Whisk the remaining 1/4 cup milk into the cornstarch mixture until smooth and thoroughly blended. Slowly whisk in the hot milk mixture. Return all to the saucepan. Slowly bring to a boil over medium heat, stirring constantly. Boil gently 2 minutes, stirring constantly; the mixture should become fairly thick.

In a small bowl, whisk egg and egg yolks together. Slowly whisk in 1 cup of the thickened milk mixture. Whisk back into the rest of the mixture in the saucepan. Cook over medium heat, whisking constantly, for about 2 minutes, or until mixture becomes slightly thicker. Do not allow the mixture to boil or overcook.

Strain pudding into a clean bowl; add chocolate, butter and vanilla, whisking until smooth and chocolate is melted. Lay a sheet of waxed paper directly on the surface of pudding to prevent skin forming on top. Cool on a wire rack; then refrigerate. (Or pour into 4 glass sundae dishes, before refrigerating.) Serve chilled with a dollop of whipped cream.

Princess Rice

Jane Milza
Staten Island Advance, Staten Island, N.Y.

This recipe is a variation of the traditional rice dish known all over Scandinavia. It is a favorite with my children. The Danish friend who introduced me to it said, according to tradition, "a good mother always makes sure her youngest child gets the whole almond because the child then feels very special."

Makes 6 - 8 servings

2/3 cup uncooked rice
3 cups milk
2 envelopes unflavored gelatin
1/2 cup cold water
1/2 cup boiling water
2/3 cup granulated sugar

1/2 cup toasted slivered almonds
2 teaspoons vanilla
2 cups heavy cream, whipped
1 whole almond

In a large saucepan, combine rice and milk; cook, stirring occasionally, for 35 minutes, or until rice is cooked. Spoon rice into a bowl.

In another bowl, soften gelatin in cold water, then add boiling water and stir to dissolve gelatin. Add gelatin mixture, sugar, slivered almonds and vanilla to rice. Chill until mixture is set.

Fold in whipped cream and whole almond. Pour into individual dishes or a large glass bowl; chill again.

Serve topped with lingonberries, as the Scandinavians do, or top with a hot raspberry sauce made by thawing a package of frozen raspberries and heating them with about 1/4 cup liquid.

Creme Bruleé

Marie Bianco
Newsday, Long Island, N.Y.

Creme Bruleé sounds as if it should be a French dish, when, actually, it's British. The name, however, is French and translates as burnt cream. The creamy custard topped with burnt sugar was a specialty of Trinity College in Cambridge, where it was called Cambridge Cream in the early 18th Century.

Makes 6 servings

3 cups heavy cream
Dash salt
6 egg yolks

2/3 cup granulated sugar
1 teaspoon vanilla
6 tablespoons brown sugar

In a medium saucepan, combine cream and salt. Cook over medium heat until cream begins to simmer. Do not boil.

In a mixing bowl, combine egg yolks and sugar; stir well. Remove cream from heat. Gradually add egg yolk mixture, stirring gently until sugar dissolves. Stir in vanilla. Strain mixture into a large measuring cup. This will make it easier to pour the liquid into ramekins.

Fill 6 heat-proof ramekins (6 to 8 ounces each) with mixture and place in a large roasting pan. Place pan in oven and pour hot water halfway up the sides of the ramekins. Cover pan loosely with foil. Bake in a 300-degree oven for 1 hour and 15 minutes. Remove ramekins from oven; cool. Chill for several hours.

Before serving, preheat broiler 10 minutes. Sprinkle 1 tablespoon brown sugar evenly over tops of custards. Place ramekins, a few at a time, as close to the broiler as possible. It will take up to 2 minutes for the sugar to caramelize. Watch carefully. The dishes might have to be moved around for even browning. If not served immediately, refrigerate. However, putting the ramekins in the refrigerator for more than 3 or 4 hours will cause the sugar to liquefy.

Fruits, Cobblers & Fruitcakes

Almond-Chocolate Meringue Cakes
Blackberry Cobbler
Cranberry-Raspberry Compote with
   Yogurt Cream
Danish Pastry Apple Squares
Dialogue of Fruits
Jesse's Apple Crumble
Last-Minute Fruitcake
Mabel Ward's Fruitcake
Mac Mac's Angel Hash
Mom's Peach Cobbler
Orange Muffins
Pavlova
Peach Dumpling Roll-Ups
Pineapple Honey Rice
Rhode Island Shortcakes

Dialogue of Fruits

Phyllis Richman
The Washington Post, Washington, D.C.

This recipe was served as dessert at a dinner prepared to inaugurate Lufthansa Airlines' new Washington-Frankfurt service. I had had something similar at another dinner, but it was used instead of sorbet to refresh the palate between courses. The recipe, which originated in Germany, is as beautiful a plate as ever has been invented.

Makes 4 servings

1/2 cup water
1/2 cup granulated sugar
1 pound Bartlett pears, peeled, cored and cooked until just tender

4 kiwis, peeled and sliced
1 mango, peeled and sliced
1 papaya, peeled and sliced
16 strawberries, rinsed, drained and hulled

In a small saucepan, combine water and sugar. Bring to a boil; boil 2 minutes. Remove from heat and cool syrup thoroughly.

In a food processor fitted with the steel blade or in a blender, puree cooked pears with 1 to 3 tablespoons cooled sugar syrup, to thin the puree just enough so it doesn't run. Strain puree and chill.

Repeat this process individually with kiwis, mango, papaya and strawberries, adding just enough sugar syrup to each puree to keep it from running. Strain each puree and chill 30 minutes.

Put 2 tablespoons of each puree on 4 large, chilled serving plates, going clockwise from papaya puree to pear puree, then strawberry puree, mango puree and kiwi puree. Tap the plates lightly to spread the purees evenly, then with a fork, swirl the purees until an abstract design is achieved.

Serve as dessert with sherbet, or as a refreshment between the appetizer and main course.

Note: Other fruits such as blackberries, raspberries, ripe peaches or black currants could be substituted.

Jesse's Apple Crumble

Candy Sagon

Dallas Times Herald, Dallas, Texas

Sliced fresh apples baked with a crunchy topping made of rolled oats is easy, relatively healthy and my young son, Jesse, loves it. The topping is an adaptation of a recipe from cookbook author Maida Heatter.

Makes 6 - 8 servings

2 tablespoons granulated sugar
1/4 teaspoon ground cinnamon

Topping
1/2 cup sifted all-purpose flour
1/4 teaspoon ground nutmeg
1/4 teaspoon ground cinnamon
1/4 cup granulated sugar
1/2 cup firmly packed dark brown sugar

5 to 6 medium-size, tart apples (Winesap, McIntosh or Granny Smith)

1/2 cup unsalted butter or margarine, cold and firm, cut into pieces
1/2 cup old-fashioned rolled oats (instant oats will not turn out as crunchy)
Additional ground cinnamon

In a small bowl, combine sugar and cinnamon. Peel, core and slice apples. Layer one-third of the apple slices in a greased 9-inch square pan. Sprinkle with one-third of the cinnamon-sugar mixture. Continue layering apples and sprinkling with cinnamon-sugar mixture until all the apples are used.

To make the topping, stir together in a medium mixing bowl the flour, nutmeg, cinnamon and granulated sugar. Add the brown sugar; stir to mix. Add the butter or margarine; cut it in with a pastry blender or two knives, until the mixture resembles coarse crumbs (not too fine). Stir in the oats.

Sprinkle topping evenly over apples. Lightly sprinkle top with additional cinnamon to taste. Bake in a preheated 375-degree oven for 25 to 30 minutes, or until apples are soft. Place dish under broiler for about 1 minute to brown topping, if desired.

Serve warm, at room temperature or cold. Ice cream or whipped cream goes well as an extra touch, but this is really great by itself.

Peach Dumpling Roll-Ups

Sue Dawson
The Columbus Dispatch, Columbus, Ohio

This recipe is an updated version of old-fashioned peach dumplings. Traditionally, each peach is wrapped in its own square of pastry dough. In this version, chopped peaches are spread on a sheet of dough, then rolled up and cut like cinnamon rolls. They are especially good served warm from the oven with a dollop of whipped cream or a scoop of vanilla or peach ice cream.

Makes 8 servings

Filling

5 to 6 ripe peaches
1 tablespoon lemon juice
1 tablespoon butter or margarine, softened
1/3 cup granulated sugar
1/2 teaspoon ground cinnamon

Sugar syrup

3/4 cup granulated sugar
3/4 cup water
1-1/2 tablespoons butter or margarine
1/4 teaspoon ground cinnamon

Dough

2 cups all-purpose flour
1/2 teaspoon baking powder
1/2 teaspoon salt
1/2 cup solid shortening
1/4 cup butter or margarine, softened
5 to 6 tablespoons ice water

For the filling, peel peaches and slice. Measure 3 cups sliced peaches, then coarsely chop them on a cutting board. Return the peaches to measuring cup or medium bowl and toss them with lemon juice; set aside. (The remaining ingredients for filling will be used later.)

For the sugar syrup, combine granulated sugar with water, butter and cinnamon in a medium saucepan. Bring to a boil, stirring occasionally, then simmer for 3 minutes. Set aside.

To make the dough, combine flour, baking powder and salt in a mixing bowl. With a pastry blender, cut in the shortening and butter until mixture resembles coarse crumbs. Sprinkle in ice water, a little at a time, tossing with a fork until mixture holds together in a ball.

On a flour-dusted pastry cloth, roll out dough to a 12x10- inch rectangle. Spread with 1 tablespoon softened butter. Sprinkle with 1/3 cup granulated sugar and 1/2 teaspoon cinnamon. Drain the peaches in a sieve; spread over dough, leaving a 1- inch border all around. From the long side of the dough, roll up the dough jelly-roll fashion, using the pastry cloth to help you roll. Moisten the seam with water and pinch lightly to seal. Slice off ragged, unfilled ends of the roll. Cut remaining roll into 8 slices, about 1-1/2 inches thick.

With a spatula, lift slices and place, cut-side down, in a greased 11x7x2-inch baking pan. Leave space between the slices.

Reheat sugar syrup until hot, then pour over and around the slices.

Bake in a preheated 400-degree oven (375-degree oven, if using a glass pan) for 40 to 45 minutes, or until rolls are golden brown. Baste rolls once or twice with bubbling syrup while baking. Let cool about 10 minutes before serving. If desired, serve with whipped cream or ice cream.

Danish Pastry Apple Squares

Ellen Carlson
St. Paul Pioneer Press Dispatch, St. Paul, Minn.

Because locally grown summer and winter apples are plentiful in Minnesota, delectable apple desserts are favorites with residents of the state. I obtained this recipe many years ago from my sister-in-law who is of Scandinavian descent. When I arrived at her home in northern Minnesota after a four-hour drive, she served these "just baked and still slightly warm" bars. They were so delicious, I just had to have the recipe. Since then, I have made them many times.

Makes 15 - 25 servings

2-3/4 cups all-purpose flour
1/2 teaspoon salt
1 cup plus 2 tablespoons solid shortening
1 egg, separated
Milk

1 cup crushed cornflakes
8 cups sliced apples
1 teaspoon ground cinnamon
1/4 teaspoon ground nutmeg
2/3 cup granulated sugar

Icing
1 cup confectioners' sugar
1/2 teaspoon vanilla

1 to 2 tablespoons water

Sift flour with salt into a medium bowl; cut in shortening until particles are the size of small peas. Slightly beat the egg yolk in a measuring cup; add enough milk to yolk to make 2/3 cup liquid. Add liquid to flour mixture; toss together to make a soft dough.

Divide dough into two portions. Roll one portion of dough to fit a 15x10x1-inch jelly-roll pan. Sprinkle dough with crushed cornflakes.

Combine apples, cinnamon, nutmeg and sugar; place in a layer over cornflakes.

Roll out remaining portion of dough; place on top and pinch edges together. Beat egg white until just stiff; brush over crust.

Bake in a preheated 375-degree oven for 50 to 60 minutes, or until apples are tender and crust is golden brown.

While pastry is baking, prepare icing. Put confectioners' sugar in a medium bowl; add vanilla and enough water to make an icing of spreading consistency.

When pastry is done, remove from oven and let cool slightly. Spread icing on top while still warm.

Note: For easier handling, roll dough between pieces of waxed paper or plastic wrap.

Mom's Peach Cobbler

Lee Aschoff
Milwaukee Sentinel, Milwaukee, Wis.

This peach cobbler recipe is a favorite of mine that I used to watch my mother make. Its origins are hazy, but Mom's been making it in our house and making the kitchen smell like heaven for more than 30 years.

Makes about 9 servings

3 cups sliced fresh peaches, or more
1 cup plus 3 tablespoons granulated sugar, divided
1/2 teaspoon almond extract
1 tablespoon lemon juice
1 teaspoon grated lemon peel

1-1/2 cups all-purpose flour
1/2 teaspoon salt
1 tablespoon baking powder
1/3 cup solid shortening
1/2 cup milk
1 egg, well beaten
Vanilla ice cream (optional)

Arrange peaches in a greased 8-inch square baking pan. Sprinkle peaches with mixture of 1 cup sugar, almond extract, lemon juice and lemon peel. Heat in the preheating 400-degree oven while preparing shortcake.

Sift together flour, salt, baking powder and 1 tablespoon sugar. Cut into shortening until mixture resembles coarse crumbs. Add milk and egg all at once. Stir just enough to moisten flour.

Spread dough over hot peaches. Sprinkle with remaining 2 tablespoons sugar. Bake in preheated 400-degree oven for 35 to 40 minutes, or until done. Serve with vanilla ice cream, if desired.

Almond-Chocolate Meringue Cakes

Faye Levy

Bon Appetit magazine, Los Angeles, Calif.

This light, elegant dessert is typical of the style Californians love. It features individual almond meringues sandwiched with a chocolate filling and surrounded by a fresh strawberry sauce.

Makes 8 - 9 servings

Almond meringues

3/4 cup unblanched almonds (about 4 ounces)

2/3 cup granulated sugar, divided

1 tablespoon cornstarch

4 egg whites, at room temperature

1/8 teaspoon cream of tartar

Chocolate whipped cream

3 ounces semisweet chocolate, chopped

1 cup heavy cream, well chilled

2 teaspoons granulated sugar

1 teaspoon vanilla

Fresh strawberry sauce

6 cups fresh strawberries

About 1 cup confectioners' sugar, sifted

1 tablespoon fresh lemon juice (optional)

Additional confectioners' sugar, for garnish

8 strawberry halves, for garnish

For the almond meringues, position rack in the center of the oven and preheat to 300 degrees. Butter and lightly flour 2 nonstick baking sheets, tapping each to remove excess flour. If using regular baking sheets, lightly butter corners and line sheets with foil; butter and lightly flour foil. Using a 3-inch plain cookie cutter, mark 16 to 18 circles, spacing them about 1/2 inch apart, on prepared pans. Have ready a rubber spatula for folding and a pastry bag fitted with a 3/8-inch plain tip.

Grind almonds with 1/2 cup sugar in a food processor until as fine as possible, scraping inward occasionally. Transfer almond mixture to a medium bowl. Sift cornstarch over mixture. Using a fork, stir lightly until blended.

Using an electric mixer, beat egg whites with cream of tartar in a large dry bowl with a dry beater. Begin beating at medium speed and increase to medium-high, until whites form soft peaks. With mixer at high speed, gradually beat in remaining 2-2/3 tablespoons sugar. Continue beating until whites are just stiff and shiny, but not dry, about 15 seconds.

Sprinkle about 1/3 of the almond mixture over the whites while gently folding with a rubber spatula. Continue sprinkling and folding as gently and as quickly as possible until just blended.

Immediately transfer mixture to pastry bag, using rubber spatula. Beginning at center of 1 circle marked on baking sheet, pipe meringue in tight spiral until circle is completely covered. Use uniform pressure so spiral has an even thickness. If there are holes in spiral, pipe a small dot of meringue in each hole. Continue with remaining circles.

Bake meringues in a preheated 300-degree oven for 28 minutes. (If both baking sheets do not fit on center rack, bake them on 2 racks and switch their positions after baking 15 minutes.) Meringues are done when they are light brown, dry and just firm, but not hard. To check, touch center of each meringue very lightly. Your finger should not leave an impression. Remove one and look at the bottom. It should be golden brown; do not let meringues get darker or they will have a burnt taste.

Immediately release meringues gently from baking sheets or foil, using a large metal spatula; peel off foil, if necessary. If meringues are sticky on the bottom, reduce oven temperature to 275 degrees and return to oven until dry, about 5 more minutes. Transfer them to wire racks and cool completely. (Meringues can be kept up to 5 days in an airtight container in dry weather, or they can be frozen.)

Arrange meringues in pairs of similar size. If necessary, use the point of a sharp paring knife to carefully trim uneven edges. Put meringue pairs on a tray with 1 meringue facing up (it will be bottom meringue in each sandwich); keep its partner nearby, flat-side down.

To make the chocolate whipped cream, chill a large mixing bowl. Melt chocolate in the top of a double boiler set over hot, not boiling, water over low heat. Stir until smooth. Remove double boiler from heat, but leave chocolate over hot water.

Whip cream with sugar and vanilla in chilled bowl until stiff. Remove chocolate from above water and allow to cool 30 seconds. Quickly stir about 1/2 cup whipped cream into chocolate. As quickly as possible, fold mixture into remaining whipped cream until smooth; work quickly so chocolate does not harden upon contact with cold whipped cream.

Spoon about 1/4 cup filling onto center of each bottom meringue. Spread it to an even layer about 3/4 inch thick, adding more filling, if needed. Set top meringue, flat-side down, gently on filling. Smooth sides of filling gently, adding more filling, if necessary. Repeat with remaining meringues and filling.

Set cakes on a tray and cover gently. Refrigerate 3 hours to firm filling. For crunchy meringues, serve within 3 more hours. (Cakes still have good flavor after being refrigerated for up to 2 days, but meringues lose their crunchiness.)

To make the stawberry sauce, rinse and hull strawberries. Puree berries in food processor or blender. Add 1 cup confectioners' sugar. Process until very smooth. Taste sauce, and whisk in 1 or 2 more tablespoons confectioners' sugar, if needed. Whisk sauce thoroughly so the sugar is completely blended. Strain sauce, pressing on mixture in strainer. Add lemon juice, if desired. Cover and refrigerate 30 minutes. (Sauce can be kept, covered, 1 day in the refrigerator.) Stir before serving.

Just before serving, sift additional confectioners' sugar lightly over top of each cake, and top with half of a strawberry. Set cakes on individual dessert plates and pour strawberry sauce carefully around them.

Pavlova

Tui Flower
New Zealand Newspapers Limited, Auckland, New Zealand

Pavlova, a meringue dessert, was named after a Russian ballerina who performed in New Zealand and Australia in the early 1900s. Top it with exotic New Zealand fruits — kiwifruit, passionfruit, tamarillos or feijoas — or with the more familiar strawberries or raspberries.

Makes 6 - 8 servings

4 egg whites
1 cup granulated sugar
1/4 teaspoon salt
1 teaspoon vanilla
1 teaspoon white vinegar

Confectioners' sugar
1 cup heavy cream, whipped
Kiwifruit, strawberries, raspberries or other fresh fruit, sliced

Prepare an 8-inch springform pan by cutting a circle of waxed paper to fit the bottom. Cut a strip of waxed paper about 2 inches wider than the pan is deep and line the sides of pan with it. Grease paper well. Dip hand into cold water and shake over prepared pan.

In large bowl of electric mixer, beat egg whites until soft peaks form. Gradually add sugar and salt; continue beating until well incorporated. Add vanilla and vinegar; beat until meringue turns glossy and stiff peaks form when beater is lifted from mixture.

Turn meringue into prepared pan and spread it evenly over bottom with spatula. The top should be fairly even. Bake in preheated 350-degree oven for 15 minutes. Check Pavlova to see if it has begun to rise. If so, turn oven off and let the Pavlova sit for 1 hour if your oven retains heat well. If the Pavlova hasn't begun to rise, bake another 10 to 15 minutes at 350 degrees, and then turn the heat off for one hour. If your oven does not retain heat well, reduce heat to 175 degrees after the first 15 minutes and bake 1 hour longer.

Remove from oven and let cool. Remove from pan and put on plate dusted with confectioners' sugar. Top with whipped cream and fresh fruit.

If a free-form Pavlova is preferred, line a baking sheet with greased waxed paper or foil and turn stiffly beaten meringue into center. With a spatula, shape into a 8- or 9-inch circle. Bake and serve as directed for springform pan.

Blackberry Cobbler

Louise Durman
The Knoxville News-Sentinel, Knoxville, Tenn.

Blackberries grow wild in East Tennessee. In late June and July, it's not uncommon to see people walking along the roads picking berries. Children come door to door selling them. It also is becoming an industry in East Tennessee with cultivated blackberries being grown and sold at pick-your-own farms. The cultivated berries are thornless and easy to pick.

Many people in Tennessee call this Mountain Cobbler.

Makes 8 servings

1 quart blackberries (or peaches, strawberries or apples)
1/2 cup water
1-1/2 to 2 cups granulated sugar, divided

1 teaspoon lemon juice
1/4 cup butter or margarine
1 cup self-rising flour (see note)
1 cup milk
1/2 teaspoon ground cinnamon (optional)

Wash berries; drain well. In a large saucepan, combine berries, water and 1/2 to 1 cup sugar (to taste). Cook until mixture is hot and sugar is dissolved. Remove from heat and add lemon juice.

Melt butter in a 2-quart baking pan. Combine 1 cup sugar and flour in a medium mixing bowl. Stir in milk. Add cinnamon, if desired. Pour batter over melted butter in pan, but do not stir. Spoon berries over batter, but do not stir. (Batter will rise to top to form a crust.)

Bake in a preheated 350-degree oven for 45 minutes.

Note: If desired, use 1 cup all-purpose flour with 2 teaspoons baking powder and a dash of salt instead of the self-rising flour.

Rhode Island Shortcakes

Marian Burros
The New York Times, New York City, N.Y.

This recipe comes from Al Farno's restaurant in Providence, R.I. They make the shortcake with Johnnycake meal from Gray's Grist Mill in Adamsville, R.I., and it is the best shortcake I have ever eaten. The meal is available in 2-pound bags and in 5-pound bags from Gray's Grist Mill, P.O. Box 422, Adamsville, R.I. 02801.

Makes 6 - 8 shortcakes

1-1/2 cups all-purpose flour
1/2 cup Johnnycake meal
3 tablespoons granulated sugar
4 teaspoons baking powder

4 tablespoons cold, unsalted butter, cut into 12 pieces
1 cup heavy cream

Raspberry puree
1/2 pint fresh raspberries
1 to 2 tablespoons superfine sugar

1 to 2 tablespoons raspberry juice

Combine flour, cake meal, sugar and baking powder in the bowl of a food processor fitted with a steel blade. Pulse on and off to combine. Add the butter. Pulse on and off 18 to 20 times to combine.

Empty into a mixing bowl. Stir in the cream with a fork, just until blended. Turn out on a pastry board and knead a few times.

Press dough into a square 1 to 1-1/4 inches thick. Cut into 6 or 8 squares. Place the squares on a lightly greased cookie sheet. Bake in a preheated 425-degree oven for 15 to 20 minutes, or until golden. Cool 15 minutes before serving.

Meanwhile, prepare raspberry puree by putting berries in a blender or food processor. Add sugar and liquid. Blend. Strain, if desired.

At serving time, split each shortcake and fill with raspberry puree.

Note: Shortcakes can be baked a few hours ahead of time, cooled completely, then wrapped in aluminum foil. To serve, reheat in foil in a 350-degree oven for about 10 minutes.

Cranberry-Raspberry Compote

Evelyn Wavpotich
The Island Packet, Hilton Head Island, S.C.

My family reserves this easy-to-prepare dessert for festive occasions. The yogurt topping also will dress up a dish of gelatin dessert or add a royal touch to chocolate pudding.

Makes 8 servings

1 package (8 or 10 ounces) frozen raspberries, thawed
2 cups fresh or frozen cranberries
1/2 cup granulated sugar
3 tablespoons cranberry juice cocktail
Yogurt Cream (recipe follows)
Fresh mint sprigs (optional)

Puree raspberries in a food processor or blender. Sieve in strainer to remove seeds. In a medium saucepan, combine raspberry puree with cranberries; simmer, covered, for about 5 minutes, or until cranberries are tender. Gently stir in sugar and juice. Chill.

Serve in parfait glasses topped with Yogurt Cream and garnished with mint.

Yogurt Cream

Makes about 2 cups

1 cup vanilla yogurt
1/2 cup heavy cream, whipped

In a medium mixing bowl, stir yogurt to soften. Then fold in whipped cream. Chill before serving.

Use to top Cranberry-Raspberry Compote or other desserts.

Last-Minute Fruitcake

Dolores Kostelni
Lexington, Va.

My family likes this fruitcake better than the regular glacé fruitcake. It is easy to do.

Makes 20 - 24 servings

1 pound dried figs
1 pound dried, pitted dates (not sugared)
8 to 10 ounces dried apricots
2 cups chopped walnuts or pecans
1 cup slivered almonds
3 cups unsweetened orange juice
3 cups all-purpose unbleached flour
2 teaspoons baking soda
1/2 teaspoon salt
2 teaspoons ground cinnamon
2 teaspoons grated nutmeg
1/2 cup granulated sugar
2 cups water
1 cup unsalted butter
2 cups firmly packed dark brown sugar
2 teaspoons vanilla
4 eggs, beaten

Cut figs, dates and apricots into skinny strips or small pieces with a pair of kitchen scissors or a knife. In a large mixing bowl, combine cut-up dried fruits, walnuts and almonds. Add orange juice; mix well. Cover bowl and allow mixture to stand 3 days in a cool spot outside the refrigerator, if possible.

On the baking day, sift together flour, baking soda, salt, cinnamon and nutmeg. Combine 1 cup of the flour mixture with the fruit mixture. (All liquid will have been absorbed, so there is no need to drain fruit mixture.)

In a medium saucepan, combine granulated sugar and water; bring to a boil. Add butter and brown sugar; cook over medium heat until butter is melted. Remove from heat and cool to room temperature. Add vanilla and eggs. Pour over fruit mixture. Add remaining flour mixture; mix well with hands or a wooden spoon.

Pour batter into a greased and floured 10-inch tube pan or into 3 greased and floured 9x5x3-inch loaf pans. Bake in a preheated 350-degree oven for 60 to 70 minutes, or until toothpick inserted near the center comes out clean. Let cake cool 15 to 20 minutes before removing from pan. Cool completely on a wire rack. Store in an airtight container.

Mabel Ward's Fruitcake

Barbara Gibbs Ostmann
St. Louis Post-Dispatch, St. Louis, Mo.

This is a fruitcake for people who don't usually like fruitcake — there's no citron and no booze. The recipe is from Mabel Ward of St. Clair, Mo. She got the recipe from her sister in New York who got it from their sister in Georgia. I received it at a church gathering and promptly went home and tried it. It's not cheap — the ingredients cost about $30 — but it's worth every cent.

This fruitcake has almost no cake at all — there is only one cup of flour in the recipe. It is a wonderful concoction of nuts and fruits.

Makes 4 loaves

2 cans (3-1/2 ounces each) flaked coconut (or one 7-ounce bag)
2 pounds pitted dates, chopped
1 pound candied cherries, coarsely chopped
1 pound candied pineapple, coarsely chopped
1 pound pecans, coarsely chopped (or use pecan halves)
1 pound English walnuts or brazil nuts, coarsely chopped
1 cup all-purpose flour
2 cans (14 ounces each) sweetened condensed milk (not evaporated milk)

In a large bowl or other container, combine the coconut, dates, cherries, pineapple, pecans and walnuts. Sift flour over the mixture; stir to mix well. Add sweetened condensed milk; mix well. Mixture will be very thick and stiff.

Grease four 9x5x3-inch loaf pans. Line with waxed paper, leaving a 2-inch overhang of paper. (If desired, grease the waxed paper, too.) Pack mixture into pans lightly. Bake in a 300-degree oven for 1 hour. Cool on wire racks.

While cakes are still warm, turn out of pans and remove paper. If cake sticks to paper, return to oven for a few minutes. Store cakes in airtight containers.

Note: You can use the food processor to chop the dates, cherries, pineapple, pecans and walnuts. The dates must be processed in small batches to prevent overworking the motor. Add some of the flour or throw in a handful of nuts with each batch of dates. You must have something dry (the flour or nuts) to coat the sticky dates as they are chopped. Use the same procedure for the cherries and pineapple. Be careful not to overprocess the fruit. You can purchase chopped dates, but they are usually sugar-coated and could make the end product too sweet.

This fruitcake is ready to eat immediately.

Mac Mac's Angel Hash

Louis Mahoney
The Richmond News Leader, Richmond, Va.

The sweet-sour smell of this custard signaled Christmas, the only time it was served, at my grandmother's house in North Carolina.

Makes 18 - 24 servings

2 cups granulated sugar
About 1/2 cup distilled white vinegar
3 eggs, very well beaten
1 can (15-1/2 ounces) crushed pineapple in natural juice, well drained

1 pound marshmallows (see note)
2 cups heavy cream, whipped
1/2 pound sliced almonds, toasted, divided

Note: You can use miniature marshmallows, but the texture is better if you use regular-size marshmallows and snip them into quarters with kitchen scissors.

Place sugar in the top of a double boiler. Add just enough vinegar to moisten sugar, about 1/2 cup. Thoroughly mix in eggs. Cook, stirring, over simmering water, until a thick, smooth custard forms, 20 to 30 minutes. Remove from heat and let stand until cooled to room temperature.

In a large mixing bowl, stir together cooled custard, drained pineapple, marshmallows (cut into quarters), cream and half of the toasted almonds.

Spoon into a large crystal compote. Chill until serving time. Top with remaining toasted almonds.

Pineapple Honey Rice

Claire Barriger
The Leader-Post, Regina, Saskatchewan, Canada

The first time I tasted Pineapple Honey Rice was at a progressive dinner in a small Saskatchewan town in the '30s. The original recipe called for sugar, but I prefer to use honey. The recipe is easy to prepare, but elegant enough for special dinners.

Makes 12 - 15 servings

3 cups cooked long-grain rice
  (about 1 cup uncooked rice)
1 can (15-1/2 ounces) crushed
  pineapple, drained

1/2 cup honey
1 cup heavy cream, whipped

While rice is hot, stir in drained pineapple and honey. Cool to room temperature, then fold in whipped cream. Transfer to serving dish. Chill until ready to serve.

Orange Muffins

Loretta Scott
The Press-Enterprise, Riverside, Calif.

This is a Southern California favorite that is served at Edwards Mansion, a restaurant in Redlands, Calif. These muffins make a tasty finale for lunch or brunch.

Makes 16 muffins

2 cups sifted all-purpose flour
2/3 cup granulated sugar
1 tablespoon baking powder
2/3 cup solid shortening
1/3 cup butter, softened

4 eggs, beaten
1/2 cup milk
1/2 cup orange juice
1/2 cup diced orange sections
1/4 cup slivered almonds

In a large mixing bowl, combine flour, sugar and baking powder. One at a time, add and mix in shortening, butter, beaten eggs, milk and orange juice. Do not overmix.

Pour batter into greased or paper-lined muffin tins, filling each two-thirds full. Top each muffin with diced orange sections and slivered almonds. Bake in a preheated 350-degree oven for 25 minutes, or until done.

Ice Creams

Cherry Pineapple Ice Cream
Cranberry Sherbet
Grandpa Cahoon's Apricot Ice Cream
Frozen Sundae Pie
Lemon Cream Sherbet
Lemon Custard Ice Cream
Peach Ice Cream
Snow Ice Cream
Spiced Persimmon Ice Cream
Spicy Pumpkin Ice Cream Squares
Strawberry Ice Cream

Cherry Pineapple Ice Cream
Donna Morgan
The Salt Lake Tribune, Salt Lake City, Utah

This is a marvelous homemade ice cream with a very creamy texture.

Makes 1 gallon

1 can (8 ounces) crushed pineapple, undrained
1 jar (4 ounces) maraschino cherries, chopped
3-1/2 cups granulated sugar
Juice of 4 lemons

1 pint heavy cream, partly whipped
2 cans (12 ounces each) evaporated milk, chilled
About 1 quart milk

In the tub of an ice cream freezer, combine undrained crushed pineapple, chopped cherries and cherry liquid, sugar, lemon juice, heavy cream and evaporated milk. Add enough milk to fill the container two-thirds full. Mix well. Freeze according to manufacturer's directions.

Cranberry Sherbert
Donna Morgan
The Salt Lake Tribune, Salt Lake City, Utah

This is superb during the holidays when served as an accompaniment to roast turkey.

Makes about 1 quart

1 pound cranberries
2 cups water
2 cups granulated sugar

2 teaspoons unflavored gelatin
2 tablespoons cold water
2 cups ginger ale

In a medium saucepan, cook cranberries in water until the skins burst. Run through a food mill. Put pulp and juice in a large mixing bowl; add sugar and stir to dissolve sugar. Soften gelatin in cold water; add to cranberry mixture while still hot; stir to dissolve gelatin. Mix well. Cool, then refrigerate.

When mixture is cold, add ginger ale. Mix well. Put mixture in freezer and freeze until firm, stirring twice during the freezing time.

Peach Ice Cream

Clara Eschmann
Macon Telegraph and News, Macon, Ga.

As children, my sister, Leila, and I used to take turns winding or cranking the churn. We were always reward-ed with the dasher. Daddy would invariably caution Mother to "leave plenty on the dasher for our girls." Of course, we got hearty servings later for dessert.

Makes about ½ gallon

1 quart Custard Sauce (recipe follows)
1 cup heavy cream

4 cups mashed peaches
Juice of 1 lemon
Granulated sugar, to taste

In the tub of an ice cream freezer, combine Custard Sauce, cream, peaches and lemon juice. Mix well. Sweeten with sugar. Freeze according to manufacturer's directions.

Custard Sauce

Makes about 1 quart

6 to 8 egg yolks
1/2 cup granulated sugar
1/4 teaspoon salt

4 cups milk
2 teaspoons vanilla

In a large saucepan or the top of a double boiler, beat egg yolks slightly. Add sugar and salt. Scald milk; pour into egg yolk mixture. Cook over low heat or over simmering water in a double boiler. Stir constantly; never let the mixture boil. Cook until custard coats a spoon.

Remove from heat immediately and pour into a bowl to cool. Add vanilla or other flavoring.

Use to make Peach Ice Cream.

Note: This sauce also can be used as a topping for cakes or steamed puddings.

Grandpa Cahoon's Apricot Ice Cream

Barbara Goldman
Deseret News, Salt Lake City, Utah

Utah is a great state for homemade ice cream. This recipe has been in the Utah family of Marion Cahoon, a recipe tester for the Deseret News, for a long time. Cahoon grew up with two large apricot trees on either side of her playhouse. The trees kept the family well supplied with apricots. This ice cream is just one of the tasty apricot treats the family made.

Makes about 5 quarts

4 cups granulated sugar
Freshly squeezed juice of 3 lemons
Freshly squeezed juice of 4 oranges

1 can (12 ounces) evaporated milk
2 cups heavy cream
1 quart apricot nectar
1-3/4 quarts whole milk (see note)

In the container of an ice cream freezer, combine sugar, lemon juice, orange juice, evaporated milk, heavy cream, apricot nectar and milk. Mix well. Churn until frozen, following manufacturer's instructions.

Note: If a richer ice cream is desired, increase the heavy cream to 1 quart and reduce whole milk to 1 quart.

Snow Ice Cream

Jann Malone
Richmond Times-Dispatch, Richmond, Va.

Snow ice cream is for kids of all ages. This recipe comes from a Richmond radio station, WRVA, whose announcers give it out whenever it snows. I like it best made with brown sugar and cream. Just remember to make sure that the snow is clean.

Makes 8 servings

1 egg (optional)
1/2 cup brown or granulated sugar

1 teaspoon vanilla
1/2 cup milk or cream
2 quarts clean snow

In a medium mixing bowl, combine egg, sugar, vanilla and milk. Put snow in a large bowl and pour egg mixture over it. Stir quickly, before the snow melts. Taste and add more sugar and vanilla, if needed.

Editors' note: Eating snow is not recommended by some health agencies because of the possibility of contamination of snow by lead in the air.

Lemon Cream Sherbet

Mary Lou Montgomery
Hannibal Courier-Post, Hannibal, Mo.

This recipe appeared in our newspaper on a hot June day. I thought the recipe sounded good and went home and made it. I loved it and have made it many times since. It is easy to make, will keep for several weeks in the freezer and is suitable for family or as an elegant dessert.

Makes 6 servings

3 egg whites
1 cup plus 2 tablespoons
  granulated sugar, divided
1 cup heavy cream

2 cups milk
Grated rind of 1 lemon
Juice of 2 lemons

In a small bowl, beat egg whites until foamy. Add 2 tablespoons sugar and continue beating until soft peaks form. Do not overbeat. In another bowl, beat cream until soft peaks form.

In a large bowl, combine milk, lemon rind, lemon juice and remaining 1 cup sugar; mix well. Fold in beaten egg whites and whipped cream.

Pour into a 13x9x2-inch pan. Put in freezer and let partly freeze. Beat partly frozen sherbet with an electric mixer until smooth and fluffy. Cover and return to freezer. This can be prepared several days in advance.

Lemon Custard Ice Cream

Donna Morgan
The Salt Lake Tribune, Salt Lake City, Utah

*This has been my family's favorite ice cream recipe
for more than 15 years. It's very creamy and custardy.
It's great with brownies.*

Makes 1 gallon

2 quarts milk
4 cups granulated sugar
2 heaping tablespoons all-
purpose flour
5 eggs, well beaten
1 quart heavy cream

1 can (12 ounces) evaporated
milk
2 tablespoons vanilla
1 teaspoon lemon extract
Dash salt

In a large saucepan, heat milk. Combine sugar and flour; add
to milk. Add eggs before milk gets too hot. Cook slowly until thick,
stirring constantly. Cool.

Add cream, evaporated milk, vanilla, lemon extract and salt
to cooled mixture. Pour into the tub of an ice cream freezer and
freeze according to manufacturer's directions.

Strawberry Ice Cream

Elaine Corn
Sacramento Bee, Sacramento, Calif.

I used to live in Louisville, Ky., and every year I gave a Derby party. I always had two ice cream makers going and this recipe for stawberry ice cream was always in one of them.

Makes 20 small servings

1 cup water
1-1/4 cups granulated sugar, divided
1 quart whole strawberries, washed and hulled, plus 1-1/2 cups sliced strawberries, divided
Juice of 1 large lemon

1-1/2 cups heavy cream
1-1/2 cups half-and-half or light cream
1 vanilla bean
6 egg yolks
6 tablespoons butter, softened, cut into pieces

Make a simple syrup by combining water and 1/4 cup sugar in a small saucepan. Bring to a boil; remove from heat and cool. Soak whole strawberries in the sugar syrup. Chill, stirring now and then, until ready to use.

In a large saucepan, combine the 1-1/2 cups sliced strawberries, 1/4 cup granulated sugar and lemon juice. Heat to boiling, breaking up berries. Add cream, half-and-half and vanilla bean. Bring to a boil, remove from heat and let stand 10 minutes. Give mixture a stir halfway through cooling.

In a bowl, beat the egg yolks and remaining 3/4 cup granulated sugar until light yellow and mixture ribbons over itself when dropped from a whisk. Add a little of the cooked strawberry mixture to the yolks. Then add the yolks to the strawberry mixture in the pan. Return pan to medium heat and cook until foamy and thick, but do not allow mixture to boil.

Remove from heat. Whisk in butter, pat by pat. Allow this custard mixture to cool to room temperature, then cover with plastic wrap and chill overnight, or for as long as 3 days.

Just before freezing, scrape vanilla bean's seeds into chilled custard; remove the bean. Freeze in an ice cream freezer according to manufacturer's directions until semi-firm. Drain whole strawberries well and add to freezer during final 15 minutes of freezing.

Spicy Pumpkin Ice Cream Squares

Louise Tennent Smith
Columbus Ledger-Enquirer, Columbus, Ga.

At Thanksgiving and Christmas, we usually have a full table. The guests often offer to contribute a dish to the feast, and their contributions are usually special treats. This lovely twist on the traditional Thanksgiving pumpkin dessert, which Pamela Stacy contributed one year, has become a family favorite. Not only is it good, but it can be made in advance in a jiffy.

Makes 18 servings

1 can (16 ounces) canned pumpkin (about 2 cups)
1 cup granulated sugar
1 teaspoon salt
1 teaspoon ground ginger
1 teaspoon ground cinnamon
1/2 teaspoon ground nutmeg

1 cup toasted chopped pecans
1/2 gallon vanilla ice cream, softened
36 gingersnaps
Whipped cream and pecan halves, for garnish

In a mixing bowl, combine pumpkin, sugar, salt, ginger, cinnamon and nutmeg. Fold in pecans. In a chilled bowl, fold pumpkin mixture into ice cream.

Line the bottom of a 13x9x2-inch pan with half of the gingersnaps; top with half of the ice cream mixture. Repeat layers. Freeze until firm, about 5 hours. Cut into squares. Garnish with whipped cream and pecan halves.

Spiced Persimmon Ice Cream

Marge Hanley
The Indianapolis News, Indianapolis, Ind.

You can't have anything much more Hoosier than persimmons. Almost every farm in southern Indiana has at least one wild persimmon tree. And if you don't know a friendly tree, you can buy frozen pulp in many farm markets and some supermarkets.

I developed this recipe after tasting something similar at Peter's Restaurant — one of two top New American cuisine spots in downtown Indianapolis. I took this ice cream along with a pie to a Thanksgiving potluck several years ago. Everyone wanted the ice cream instead of the pie.

Makes about 1 quart

3 eggs
3/4 cup granulated sugar
2 cups milk (or part half-and-half and part milk)
1/4 cup persimmon puree
1/4 teaspoon ground cinnamon
Generous 1/8 teaspoon ground ginger
Generous 1/8 teaspoon freshly grated nutmeg
1 cup heavy cream
2 teaspoons vanilla

In a heavy stainless steel or anondized aluminum saucepan or in the top of a double boiler, slightly beat eggs. Beat in sugar, then stir in milk. Over medium-low heat or hot water, cook and stir until custard mixture is thickened and coats a wooden spoon. Do not boil.

Pour custard into a large bowl. Cool, then chill in the refrigerator overnight, if desired.

When ready to make the ice cream, prepare puree by cutting very ripe persimmon into pieces and pureeing in a food mill. Measure 1/4 cup puree. Stir cinnamon, ginger and nutmeg into puree.

Stir spiced puree, heavy cream and vanilla into chilled custard, mixing well. Pour into chilled canister of ice cream freezer and freeze according to manufacturer's directions. After freezing, spoon into a covered container and place in freezer to mellow several hours before serving.

Frozen Sundae Pie

Bernie Arnold
Nashville Banner, Nashville, Tenn.

*When my children were growing up, they got to
choose their birthday menu. Two never wanted a cake.
It was always Sundae Pie — with candles, of course.
They still love it — some things you just don't outgrow!*

Makes 6 - 8 servings

2 cups finely crushed creme-
  filled chocolate sandwich
  cookies, such as Oreos
  (about 18 cookies)
1/3 cup plus 1 tablespoon
  margarine or butter, melted
2 squares (1 ounce each)
  unsweetened chocolate

1/2 cup granulated sugar
1 tablespoon butter
2/3 cup evaporated milk,
  undiluted
1 quart vanilla ice cream
1/2 cup chopped nuts
  (optional)

In a medium bowl, combine cookie crumbs and melted margarine. Press into bottom and up the sides of a 9-inch pie plate. Freeze until firm.

Meanwhile, in a medium saucepan over low heat, melt chocolate. Stir in sugar and butter. Slowly add evaporated milk and continue cooking over low heat, stirring constantly, until mixture is thickened. Chill.

Fill prepared crust with slightly softened ice cream; freeze until firm.

When ice cream has frozen, cover top of pie with chilled chocolate sauce. Sprinkle with nuts, if desired. Store in freezer until a few minutes before cutting and serving.

Candies

Buckeyes
Buttery Pecan Caramels
Chocolate Velvet Fudge
Dad's Old-Fashioned Chocolate Fudge
Hazelnut Toffee
Meme's Creamy Pralines
Mother's Divinity
Old Fashioned Hard Candy
Peanut Butter Fudge
Pulled Mints

Peanut Butter Fudge

Fran Zupan
The Columbia Record, Columbia, S.C.

*I obtained this recipe from a co-worker, Deb Wool-
ley. She brings it to office Christmas parties, and we
all love it.*

Makes about 10 dozen 1-inch squares

3 cups granulated sugar
3/4 cup butter or margarine
2/3 cup evaporated milk
4 heaping tablespoons peanut butter

1 jar (7 ounces) marshmallow cream
1 cup (or more) chopped nuts
1 teaspoon vanilla

In a medium saucepan with a heavy bottom, combine sugar, butter and milk. Bring to a rolling boil, stirring constantly. Continue to boil, stirring, for 5 minutes over medium heat. Remove from heat.

Add peanut butter; stir until peanut butter is melted and blended. Add marshmallow cream, nuts and vanilla. Stir until blended.

Pour into a greased 13x9x2-inch pan. Cool to room temperature. Cut into squares. Store in an airtight container in the refrigerator.

Note: Using this size pan makes the pieces of fudge thin — but they are rich. If you prefer thicker pieces, use a smaller pan.

Buckeyes

Jane Baker
The Phoenix Gazette, Phoenix, Ariz.

My dad, Edward Lietwiler, has become quite a good candy maker. Because he was born and raised in Ohio and now lives in Columbus, Ohio, this regional candy recipe is one of his specialties.

The candy is named after buckeyes, which are round, nut-like seeds that are dark brown with a light tan tip. Ohio is often called the Buckeye State. These candies, which taste like the popular peanut butter cups, are made to look like their namesake.

As with any candy, practice makes perfect. Dad says the secret to this recipe is freezing the peanut butter balls before coating them with chocolate.

Makes about 2 pounds of candy

Approximately 1 box (16 ounces) confectioners' sugar
1/2 cup butter, softened
1-1/4 cups creamy or chunky peanut butter

Approximately 3/4 pound semisweet dipping chocolate (available at cake decorating supply stores)

In a large mixing bowl with an electric mixer, combine about three-fourths of the sugar with butter and peanut butter. Beat until mixture is well blended. At this point, you will probably have to add a little more sugar. Generally, you will use seven-eighths of a box of sugar. You want the mixture to roll into balls without sticking to your hands, but you don't want it to be too dry.

Roll mixture into 3/4-inch balls and place balls on waxed paper-lined cookie sheets. Freeze balls until well chilled.

In the top of a double boiler over hot water, melt chocolate. Stick a toothpick in the center of a frozen peanut butter ball and dip in warm chocolate so that all but top of the ball is covered. Let excess chocolate drip back into pan. Place ball on waxed paper-lined cookie sheets. Remove toothpick. Repeat until all peanut butter balls have been dipped.

After the peanut butter balls come to room temperature, you can pinch the toothpick holes closed with your fingers and smooth the top. Store in airtight containers in a cool place.

Dad's Old-Fashioned Chocolate Fudge

Sharon Hudgins
The Stars and Stripes, West Germany

My father, Lawrence Weldon, belongs to the category of men who don't cook anything except the dishes they consider to be their "specialties."

In my father's case, one of his specialties is chocolate fudge. He has made this fudge for 45 years without a formal recipe, judging how to mix and treat the ingredients merely by their look and feel.

Recently I asked him to make up a batch of this fudge, measuring each ingredient and writing down every step of the procedure as he cooked. He sent me a very well-written recipe, which concluded with the following statement: "It makes 64 one-inch pieces of candy, which serves two people, the way I eat fudge."

Makes 36 squares

4 cups granulated sugar
1/2 cup unsweetened cocoa powder
1/8 teaspoon salt
1-1/8 cups light cream or half-and-half

1 tablespoon light corn syrup
2 tablespoons butter
1-1/2 teaspoons vanilla
1-1/2 cups chopped pecans or walnuts

Butter the inside of a large (4-quart) heavy-bottomed saucepan. Combine the sugar, cocoa and salt in the pan; stir to mix well, so that no lumps of cocoa remain. Add the cream and corn syrup; stir to mix well.

Bring the mixture to a full rolling boil over medium-low heat, stirring constantly. After the mixture reaches a full rolling boil, let it cook for 3 minutes longer, stirring gently to keep it from sticking and burning. Do not scrape the sides of the pan.

At the end of 3 minutes, remove the pan from the heat. Drop 1/2 teaspoonful of the hot mixture into a cup of ice water. If it forms a slightly firm ball in the water, the fudge is ready to cool. If it doesn't form a slightly firm ball, return the pan to the heat and boil for 1 minute longer. Test again by dropping a small portion of the hot mixture into ice water. Depending on the humidity, altitude and the temperature of your stove, you might have to cook the mixture a bit longer. (If you are using a candy thermometer, the temperature of the mixture should reach 240 degrees.)

Place 2 tablespoons butter on top of the hot fudge mixture, but do not stir the mixture at all. Set the pan on a wire rack to cool, until the bottom of the pan is cool enough to touch without burning your finger. (If using a candy thermometer, the temperature of the fudge should cool to 110 degrees.)

(To cool the fudge more quickly, set the hot pan in a sink filled to a depth of 4 inches with cold water and ice cubes. Let the fudge cool until it no longer burns your tongue when you taste a spoonful of it.)

Meanwhile, butter an 8-inch square shallow baking pan.

When the fudge mixture has cooled sufficiently, stir in the vanilla, but avoid scraping the sides of the pan. Beat the mixture by hand with a large wooden spoon, just until the fudge loses its gloss and begins to thicken. Quickly stir in the chopped nuts and immediately pour the fudge into the prepared pan, smoothing it into an even layer.

Let the fudge cool to room temperature. Cut into 1-1/4 inch squares.

Note: In order to make creamy fudge and keep the fudge from "sugaring" (re-crystallizing into sugar), it is important to avoid scraping the sides of the pan once the mixture has come to a boil, and after you have taken it off the heat. Buttering the inside of the pan also helps to keep the fudge from sugaring.

Chocolate Velvet Fudge

Eleanor Ostman
St. Paul Pioneer Press-Dispatch, St. Paul, Minn.

Here's a candy recipe that all chocolate lovers should have in their recipe files.

Makes about 12 dozen 1-inch squares

4-1/2 cups granulated sugar
1 tablespoon cornstarch
1/2 teaspoon salt
1 can (12 ounces) evaporated milk
1/2 cup butter or margarine
1 package (16 ounces) regular marshmallows
1 package (12 ounces) semi-sweet chocolate morsels
1 milk chocolate candy bar (8 ounces), broken
2 teaspoons vanilla
2 cups chopped walnuts

In a heavy 5-quart Dutch oven, combine sugar, cornstarch and salt. Stir in evaporated milk and butter. Cook over medium heat, stirring constantly, until mixture comes to a rolling boil. Boil 8 minutes, stirring frequently. Remove from heat.

Stir in marshmallows, chocolate morsels, milk chocolate and vanilla; beat until smooth. Stir in walnuts.

Pour into a buttered 15x10x1-inch jelly-roll pan. Cool. Cut into squares. Store in an airtight container in the refrigerator.

Pulled Mints

Jane Baker
The Phoenix Gazette, Phoenix, Ariz.

There are many advantages to living in a Sun Belt state, but one disappointment is never being able to make these candies. When I was a kid growing up in Ohio, my dad, Edward Lietwiler, worked his magic making these mints. The weather had to be just right — cold, but not too cold, and dry. Dad says, "It is the most frustrating recipe I ever tried to make, but when they are right, they are superb."

Makes about 36 pieces

1 cup granulated sugar
1/4 cup butter
1/2 cup boiling water
Wintergreen or peppermint extract
Red or green food coloring

Butter a large platter and put it in the refrigerator. If you have a marble slab, that is even better because it is always cold.

Put sugar and butter in a large saucepan with a heavy bottom. Pour boiling water into pan. Stir until sugar dissolves, but never stir after the mixture starts to boil. Cook to 256 degrees with a candy thermometer (always use a thermometer). Carefully pour sugar mixture onto prepared, chilled platter.

Put the platter with sugar mixture outside to cool. (The outside temperature has to be below 32 degrees, but not much colder than 20 degrees.) If the candy starts to harden around the edges, pull the edges into the center.

When mixture is cool enough to handle, add a drop or two of wintergreen or peppermint extract and a few drops of coloring (red or green — just enough to make a pastel color). Then start to pull the candy. Pick it up in your hands and stretch it back and forth. (You must do the pulling outdoors.) In the beginning the candy is very soft and you cannot do much with it, but as it cools you should be able to stretch it out to almost a yard. Try to keep it the same width when you pull, or narrow sections will cool too fast and break. As you pull the candy, it will become stiffer and stiffer. Only experience can tell you exactly how long to pull.

Finally, pull candy into a long cord, then place the cord on a piece of waxed paper and snip it into 1/2-inch pieces with scissors. (You can move inside to do this.)

Let candy cool. Store in an airtight container. Separate each layer of candy with waxed paper. The candy will be very hard at this point. Store in the refrigerator overnight. In the morning the candy should be soft and smooth, but it takes a little practice to make it perfect.

Buttery Pecan Caramels

Eleanor Ostman
St. Paul Pioneer Press-Dispatch, St. Paul, Minn.

*I've made these candies for the past half-dozen years
as part of my Christmas calorie collection. The recipe,
which originally came from the local dairy council, has
never failed on me. My sister-in-law would rather have
a plate of these than any Christmas present I could buy.*

Makes 64 candies

2 cups granulated sugar
2 cups half-and-half or light cream, divided
3/4 cup light corn syrup

1/2 cup butter
1/2 cup semisweet chocolate morsels, melted
64 pecan halves

In a heavy 4-quart saucepan, combine sugar, 1 cup half-and-half, corn syrup and butter. Cook over medium heat, stirring occasionally, 7 to 8 minutes, or until mixture comes to a full boil. Add remaining 1 cup half-and-half; continue cooking, stirring often, until mixture reaches 245 degrees on a candy thermometer, or until a small amount of mixture dropped into ice water forms a firm ball. (This will take 35 to 40 minutes.)

Pour into a buttered 8-inch square pan. Cover and refrigerate 1 to 1-1/2 hours to cool.

When cool, remove from refrigerator and loosen the entire block of caramel from the pan and put it on a cutting board. Use a knife with a long blade to cut caramel into 64 squares.

Drop 1/4 teaspoon melted chocolate on top of each caramel; press pecan half into chocolate. Store candy in airtight container in refrigerator.

Note: For a slightly softer caramel, cook to just under 240 degrees.

Meme's Creamy Pralines

Jann Malone
Richmond Times-Dispatch, Richmond, Va.

When my Grandmother Malone lived in New Orleans, she learned to make pralines. Her version is creamy, as opposed to another type that has a sugary texture. Both varieties are sold in New Orleans. If you ever want to buy some, pronounce them "prawleens", not "praylines" — no one will know you're a tourist.

Makes about 2 dozen

3 cups granulated sugar
1 cup buttermilk
1 teaspoon baking soda
1-1/2 cups pecans

1 teaspoon vanilla
3 tablespoons margarine (or less)

Put sugar into a large pot, at least 3 quarts. As it cooks, the candy will bubble up to 3 or 4 times its original volume.

Mix the buttermilk and baking soda; add to sugar. Stir until well mixed.

Using a candy thermometer, cook the mixture slowly until it reaches 234 degrees. If you don't have a thermometer, cook it to the soft ball stage (when a small quantity of the mixture is dropped into ice water, it forms a ball that flattens out on its own when picked up with the fingers).

Just before that point, add the pecans. When the mixture reaches 234 degrees, remove the pot from the heat; add vanilla and margarine.

Let the mixture cool a bit, then stir vigorously until it begins to stiffen. Drop onto waxed paper by the teaspoonful. These are very rich, so it is best to make them small.

Mother's Divinity

Fran Zupan
The Columbia Record, Columbia, S.C.

My mother, Betty Haugen, who now lives in Texas but is originally from Camilla, Ga., makes this recipe for me every Christmas. She wraps each piece of candy in red and green tissue paper and stores them in a coffee can.

She does have some words of wisdom for anyone trying to make divinity: Use a tabletop mixer, not a portable one; use a wooden spoon for stirring until the sugar mixture boils; set a timer for five minutes for beating in the sugar syrup; and always use a candy thermometer attached to the side of the pan. We would add, don't try to make divinity when the humidity is high.

Makes 3 - 4 dozen pieces

2 cups granulated sugar
1/2 cup light corn syrup
1/2 cup hot water
1/4 teaspoon salt

2 egg whites
1 teaspoon vanilla
1/2 cup chopped nuts
(optional)

In a 2-quart saucepan, combine sugar, corn syrup, water and salt. Cook and stir until sugar is dissolved and mixture comes to a boil. Cook to the hard ball stage (250 degrees on a candy thermometer) without stirring. Wipe crystals from the side of the pan now and then with a fork wrapped in a damp cloth. Remove sugar mixture from heat. (Sugar mixture will string to about 12 inches.)

Using a tabletop mixer with a large mixing bowl, immediately beat egg whites until stiff. Pour hot syrup slowly over beaten whites, beating constantly at high speed for 5 minutes. Add vanilla and beat until mixture forms soft peaks and begins to lose its gloss. Add chopped nuts, if desired.

Drop from a teaspoon, pushing candy off with a second spoon onto cookie sheets covered with waxed paper. Twirl the top of each candy. If divinity becomes too stiff for twirling, add a few drops of hot water.

Hazelnut Toffee

Barb Durbin
The Oregonian, Portland, Oregon

The Pacific Northwest is a big hazelnut growing territory. (You might know these nuts by the name of filberts.) This recipe was submitted by one of our readers, Joan Harris, several years ago as part of a monthly recipe contest. I liked the recipe and have made it at home. It makes a good and very easy toffee.

Makes about 3 dozen pieces

2 cups chopped toasted hazelnuts, divided (see instructions for toasting nuts below)

1/2 cup butter (not margarine)

1/2 cup plus 1 tablespoon granulated sugar

2 tablespoons water

1-1/2 milk chocolate bars (1.65 ounces each), broken into squares

Spread 1 cup chopped nuts over bottom of an 8-inch square baking pan.

Melt butter slowly in a heavy skillet. Add sugar and water to melted butter. Stirring constantly over high heat, bring the mixture to a full boil. Cook and stir until mixture turns light brown, about 5 minutes. Mixture will mass together in sheets. Immediately pour over chopped nuts in the pan. Spread evenly to sides of pan.

Put chocolate squares over hot toffee. When chocolate is melted, spread evenly over toffee. Allow to cool at room temperature. Chocolate will be soft. Cover with remaining 1 cup chopped nuts. Press nuts into chocolate. Chill.

Break toffee into small pieces for serving. Store in a closed container in the refrigerator or freeze.

To toast hazelnuts: Spread nuts in a single layer on a large cookie sheet. Toast in a 300-degree oven for 30 minutes. Allow to cool, then rub off skins between terry cloth towels. Chop to medium grind in food processor.

Note: Other nuts can be substituted for the hazelnuts in this recipe.

Old-Fashioned Hard Candy

Barbara Gibbs Ostmann
St. Louis Post-Dispatch, St. Louis, Mo.

This recipe is from a story I wrote about a group of local women who get together each year for a candy-making session at the beginning of the holiday season. They pool their time, efforts and ingredients to make numerous batches of hard candy, which they then divide.

More than a few candy-making sessions were started by other groups of friends as a result of the article, and even some money-making projects by local church groups.

The candy itself is simple, but to get a variety of colors and flavors, a lot of batches are needed. That is why a "work session" with friends is such a good way to do it.

The only hard-to-find ingredient is the flavoring oils. They usually can be purchased in drugstores, cake decorating shops or candy stores.

Makes about 2¼ pounds

3-3/4 cups granulated sugar
1-1/4 cups light corn syrup
1 cup water
1 teaspoon flavoring oil, of choice (see note)

Food color, of choice (either paste or liquid)
Confectioners' sugar

In a heavy 3-quart saucepan, combine granulated sugar, corn syrup and water. Stir over medium heat until sugar dissolves. Brush insides of pan with water to wash down any sugar crystals.

Boil, without stirring, until temperature reaches 310 degrees on a candy thermometer, or until drops of syrup form hard, brittle threads in cold water.

Remove pan from heat. After boiling has ceased, stir in flavoring oil and coloring. Carefully pour candy (it is very hot) in thin, even strips onto heavy-duty aluminum foil that has been generously dusted with confectioners' sugar. Let cool.

Break candy strips into bite-size pieces. Store in airtight containers. (Candy will keep for several months.)

Note: The brand of flavoring oils most commonly used is Lorann Oils. The 1 dram bottle equals 1 teaspoon.

Index